SUPERNATURAL LIVING

DANIEL ADAMS

To:

From: *[signature]*

change the world for

Jesus!!!

Library of Congress Cataloging-in-Publication Data

Front cover image by Annette Groves
Book design by Annette Groves

Book Contributed by Annette Groves
Foreword by Vladimir Savchuk

DISCLAIMER

All Scripture quotations, unless indicated, are taken from the New King James Version.

BOOKBABY
Printed in the United States of America

First Printing Edition, 2022

ISBN: 978-1-66787-622-1

www.thesupernaturallife.org

I dedicate this book to my TSNL forerunners.

Contents

Foreword by Vladimir Savchuk i

Introduction 1

SUPERNATURAL LIVING

Seeing in the Spirit 5

How to Use Faith 21

How to Hear God's Voice 31

Overcoming Offense 49

Understanding the Anointing 59

How to Know If You Have a Demon 77

How to Do Self-deliverance 93

How to Overcome the Fear of Man 99

How to Avoid Sin 115

How to Live in the Spirit 127

FOREWORD
BY VLADIMIR SAVCHUK

L ike many people, I first met Daniel Adams through his YouTube videos. I saw a young man full of faith and boldness going where few dared to go and demonstrating the power of the gospel. Whether at a birth-day party, on the beach, on the street, or in church, people would encounter the Holy Spirit in a way that was visible. I had a chance to host him at HungryGen to see him operate in the power of God in close proximity. He is the real deal.

Something about Daniel that every reader will pick up on is the realness that he carries. Daniel is real about his past mistakes. It serves as a reminder to every young minister about the importance of character that goes along with the gifting. It takes humility to be real and raw.

Daniel is as bold as a lion. It takes courage to operate in the power of the Holy Spirit. So many people desire to live a supernatural life, but they lack the faith to release it. This book will equip you to activate that faith and take risks for God. To know the Holy Spirit is as important as knowing the secrets of walking in His supernatural power. This book will give you those strategies.

In Daniel 11:32 it says, "Those who do wickedly against the covenant he shall corrupt with flattery; but the people who know their God shall be strong and carry out great exploits." We live in a day and age where there is great wickedness in the world. God is building an army of wild men and women of God who will know their Lord and do great exploits. This book will give you the tools to know God and take bold action for Him.

INTRODUCTION

Many people wonder what it means to live a supernatural life. There was a time in my life where everything seemed okay to the world's eyes, but internally I was filled with turmoil. I came from a broken home; divorced parents that dragged me in and out of court as a child. My mom was a Christian, but I never saw her walking in the power of God. I did not see a difference between a Christian family and an unbelieving one. I saw my parent's struggles and in turn that filled me with pain and anger. This is what prompted me to become an MMA Cage fighter.

In 2012 I was about to have my first ever pro-fight. One night I sat down in my bed and noticed the Bible laying close by. This is the same Bible that followed me everywhere since I got saved as a child at a Baptist Church. I could not seem to shake off that Bible. I decided to open it and read. As I read, the answer became clear to me. Not only did Jesus heal the sick, cast out devils and raise the dead, but His disciples did great works as well! To top it all off, Jesus said we would do greater works than He did. He commanded us to make disciples of all nations. As this revelation hit me, I went to my computer, logged on YouTube and looked for a worship song from Jeremy Camp called 'This Man'. As I played it, the power of God fell upon me, and tears started to stream down my face. All the rage in my heart disappeared as the love of God poured into me. As a result, the next day I was holding back on my punches during practice because I did not want to hurt people any longer. For an MMA fighter, that was not a smart choice. This prompted me to switch careers and become a personal trainer.

Ever since my encounter with the Holy Spirit, a hunger was ignited within me to walk a supernatural lifestyle. One year later a woman walks into my gym looking wanting to be healed of breast cancer. No treatment was working for her, and she had heard of a personal trainer that would pray for people. What could she lose? As I began to pray for her, I was astonished at what was happening right in that moment. She assured me that each time I prayed the breast lump got smaller and smaller. Suddenly, she saw a green goo come out of her breast and disappear. The lump was completely gone! Shortly after that experience I became a full-time minister.

On my first preaching meeting in Orlando, Florida, there was a crowd of over 400 people. After the Word was preached, the power of God fell upon everybody, and mass deliverance started to take place. A Scripture that became alive to me which reads, "For the kingdom of God is not in word but in power". (New King James Version, 1 Cor. 4.20). This was just a preview of what happens when you walk in your anointing. Soon it became clear that godly character and integrity is incredibly important in your walk with God. The power came easily to me, but I had zero character. I did not deal with my issues in the beginning of my walk, and as a result I became a backslidden minister. The anointing left me, and I could not hear God's voice well any longer. I lost everything in my life, my previous marriage and previous ministry. But Jesus! One evening I was in my living room, sitting on my couch with my future wife, Heather. I was so desperate to encounter God like I did the first time back in 2012. I truly repented and asked Him for one more shot making Him a promise that I would give Him all the glory. Suddenly, I felt His presence filling every part of me. He told me that He never left and was waiting on me. I was in total awe of Him and ever since I have walked in holiness. As a result, I now have a ministry that is sparking revival in every nation.

I decided to write this book because many Christians are ignorant to the things of the Spirit. When you really tap into the things of the Spirit your world will never be the same! In this book you are going to read many different topics that are going lead you in the supernatural lifestyle. You are going to learn so much about the spirit realm, how it operates, and how things maneuver in the Spirit. My prayer is that as you read this book you will allow the Holy Spirit to teach you things and reveal mysteries that will lead you into a deeper relationship and walk with Jesus Christ. In turn, you will be activated into the supernatural life. Supernatural Living is going to lead you into a supernatural encounter with God that will leave you forever changed.

DANIEL ADAMS

SUPERNATURAL LIVING

SEEING IN THE SPIRIT

I believe many of you reading this book have probably prayed for the Lord to activate your ability to see Him. I know many people want to know how to see in the spirit. Many have asked "Daniel, how are you able to see certain things? How did you know that?" Well, the simple answer is that I prayed and asked the Holy Spirit. There was a season where I was so infatuated with people who could see in the spirit. I was almost like Godly-jealous because I wanted it so bad and I would say to myself, how are these guys doing this? What are they doing I would ask? I remember in 2013 when I was baptized in the Holy Spirit, I started to run into people who operated in the prophetic realm. I began to yearn for that ability more and more that I didn't realize that God made it so simple to see in the spirit. First, you must know where the vision is coming from. We receive several visions. For example, we all have an imagination. God uses our imagination. He uses what people call the mind's eye, not the third eye. He uses the imagination to speak. He uses the dream realm to speak. The Bible says in Joel 2:28 (NKJV), "And it shall come to pass afterwards, that I will pour out my spirit upon all flesh; and our sons and daughters shall prophesy, your old men shall dream dreams, your young men shall see visions". I believe just that; people will dream dreams and see visions. I'm going to show you a few places in the word of God where even Jesus saw in the spirit. There is also a story in the bible where Peter had a vision of animals coming down from Heaven in a blanket. You might begin praying for Jesus to activate you right now and give you the ability to see in the spirit. I can assure that this book is going to provide you such a simple path to seeing in the spirit.

There is a lot of people that want to see how the Holy Ghost sees. The Bible talks about in Matthew 13:9-16 that we have eyes to see and ears to hear.

"He who has ears to hear, let him hear!" And the disciples came and said to Him, "Why do You speak to them in parables?" He answered and said to them, "Because it has been given to you to know the mysteries of the kingdom of heaven, but to them it has not been given. For whoever has, to him more will be given, and he will have abundance; but whoever does not have, even what he has will be taken away from him. Therefore, I speak to them in parables, because seeing they do not see, and hearing they do not hear, nor do they understand. And in them the prophecy of Isaiah is fulfilled, which says: 'Hearing you will hear and shall not understand and seeing you will see and not perceive; For the hearts of this people have grown dull. Their ears are hard of hearing, and their eyes they have closed, lest they should see with their eyes and hear with their ears, lest they should understand with their hearts and turn, so that I should heal them.' But blessed are your eyes for they see, and your ears for they hear".

. – Matthew 13:9-16

The Bible also says those who have eyes to see and ears to hear what the spirit of the Lord is saying. I believe everybody has the ability to see in the spirit. Seeing in the spirit can come as a word of knowledge. In John 1:48, Jesus saw Nathaniel under the fig tree.

"Nathanael said to Him, "How do You know me?" Jesus answered and said to him, "Before Philip called you, when you were under the fig tree, I saw you."

– John 1:48

In order to properly break down this topic, I'll have to dive into what a seer is according to scripture. A seer is a person who sees in the Spirit and another name for a seer is prophet. In I Samuel 9:9, a seer was a prophet who saw visions, pictures, or scenes in the mind's eye, or dreams.

"And the servant answered Saul again and said, "Look, I have here at hand one-fourth of a shekel of silver. I will give that to the man of God, to tell us our way. (Formerly in Israel, when a man went to inquire of God, he spoke thus: "Come, let us go to the seer"; for he who is now called a prophet was formerly called a seer)".

- I Samuel 9: 8-9

Visions are pictures or scenes seen in the mind's eye. They can come in our dreams or even when our eyes are wide open. God spoke to his people through prophets in different ways, and oftentimes he spoke through visions. A seer was given insight into what God was saying by visions. The truth is, God speaks to His people through dreams and visions. As I stated previously, I used to think I would never be able to see. I was actually seeing more than I realized. I am here to tell you that you are seeing more than you know.

Now, the enemy has the ability to pervert your imagination. What you take in is what you give out. That's why it is important to read the word. It is also important to watch what goes into your ears and eyes. The enemy can play on your imagination. He can also project things to you because he knows how the human mind works. He knows how man operates because he has watched us. The devil is an ancient enemy. He knows what to do to contaminate your imagination. I can assure you that you do not want a contaminated imagination. Now, I'll give you an example. What do you think is one of the best ways to open the door to contamination? The answer is looking at the wrong things, such as sexual immorality, pornography, and things that the Lord says to stay away from in this world. Watching horror movies, death, and things like that can contaminate your imagination. Why would you watch that as Christians? If you want to see and hear from the Lord, you need to protect your temple. You need to protect your body so that your vision does not become contaminated. Guard your gates! Observe your ear gates because what comes out of a man is what contaminates him according to Matthew 15:11.

"Not what goes into the mouth defiles a man; but what comes out of the mouth, this defiles a man."– Matthew 15:11

If you wait long enough, you'll find out what people are taking in their ears and eyes. I've noticed at times that people that have lust issues will always say something perverse. People with anger or rage issues, they are quick to resort to violence and discord. Everything that is contained in the heart of man will always extend out of a man. Remember, it is not the external that defiles man, it is what comes out of him that defiles. We must remember these things in order to protect our vision. If you want to see in the spirit, protect your vision.

Now, I know people will make mistakes. I know some of us will find ourselves relaxing at a beach and suddenly you see something; a provocatively dressed woman or man for example. It is when you willingly look for it that causes issues of defilement. God also gives us grace at times because we will run into things that we cannot help. What if one day America becomes like Sodom and Gomorrah, and sexual immorality is out in the open on the streets right before our eyes? Those who are found righteous must rely on the grace of God's mercy. Ultimately, we are going to have to pray for people and the church at large. Again, it is what you are willing to let in.

The enemy is going to try to throw things in front of you, but it is the willful sin that contaminates us. We cannot control others and force anybody to do anything, but what we can do is protect ourselves. Allow Jesus Christ to lead you into all truth. So, you want to be graced to see? You must want uncontaminated eyes which means you must live a life of purity. Matthew 5:8 says "Blessed are the pure in heart, for they will see God. In Psalms 24:3-4, it talks about who can ascend into the hill of the Lord. Those with clean hands and a pure heart. Purity is the key to seeing. Take special note to "purity is the key to seeing". If you are pure, you can see like Jesus. You can see a person for how they are in the spirit. If you are contaminated, you are going look at their flesh and the flesh is what you are going see. But if you are a spiritual person, you will see the way Jesus sees, and hear the way He hears. You will talk the way Jesus talks. Remember seeing is based off the imagination. It is also profoundly based off the word of God and the truth of Jesus. If you want to see like the Lord, get to know the Lord. Additionally, when you are seeing something, the way to know if you are seeing from yourself or God is you will know it by the word of God. The Bible says my sheep know my voice and will not listen to the voice of another. This is very important. They will not see as another sees, but we should see the way Jesus sees. The Bible says those who have eyes to see let them see. Who have ears to hear? Let them hear with what the spirit of the Lord is saying.

Let us now examine word of knowledge. Word of knowledge is one of the nine gifts of the Holy Spirit which we read of in 1 Corinthians 12:1-11. The gift of word of knowledge is the supernatural revelation from God that gives you revelation about a certain situation or person. Word of knowledge is not always about knowing or a feeling, but also about seeing. In John 1:43 – 50, it says the following:

The next day Jesus decided to leave for Galilee. Finding Philip, he said to him, "Follow me. Philip, like Andrew and Peter, was from the town of Bethsaida. Philip found Nathanael and told him, "We have found the one Moses wrote about in the Law, and about whom the prophets also wrote—Jesus of Nazareth, the son of Joseph. Nazareth! Can anything good come from there?" Nathanael asked. "Come and see," said Philip. When Jesus saw Nathanael approaching, he said of him, "Here truly is an Israelite in whom there is no deceit. How do you know me?" Nathanael asked. Jesus answered, "I saw you while you were still under the fig tree before Philip called you. Then Nathanael declared, "Rabbi, you are the son of God; you are the king of Israel. Jesus said, "You believe because I told you I saw you under the fig tree. You will see greater things than that."

-        John 1:43-50

Jesus was very detailed, wouldn't you say? You see, Jesus was able to see Nathaniel sitting under a fig tree. I know some of you are thinking that is pretty cool. Now, the same spirit that raised Jesus from the dead lives inside of you. Jesus said you will do greater works. Jesus said the things you see me do; you will do also. So, what does that mean? You should be able to see people under the fig tree. You know there's been times when I'm doing ministry that the Lord will show me things people have been doing or he will show me a place that they had been. This is all to bring glory to His name. One time I saw when young man doing something upstairs in his home and I told him what I saw. I went into specific detail with him about what I saw that he immediately felt the fear of God. He couldn't believe God was seeing him in his sinful state. It brought the fear of the Lord on him, and he became repentant. Here is the beautiful thing, Jesus doesn't show us things to condemn people. He shows us things to release people from bondage which ushers them into totally victory. Think about when Jesus was talking to the woman at the well. Jesus saw that she had five husbands. He didn't acknowledge it to bring condemnation but instead to reveal to her that He is the freedom that she needs. He could have said "You are going to hell for your sins!", but he's instead he's like look, I'm standing right here to bring freedom to you through the living water that never runs dry. He allowed her to realize that He knows and sees her. God is watching us and that's a beautiful thing. We need to know the Lord so that we receive insight from Him because nothing is better than to tell somebody something that they wouldn't have expected you to know, especially when it's a complete stranger. What if we come across a stranger and began sharing what the Holy Spirit is revealing about them? It would blow their mind. You know a lot of people are scared to operate in this realm because of fear, oftentimes, afraid they will operate in the spirit of divination. Look, the only way you are going operate in the wrong capacity is if you are contaminated and in an unrepentant state; therefore, you will be operating in a perverted gift. If you truly love the Lord, which means you are not willfully sinning, prideful and trying to show-off the gift, then the Lord is able to use you. He will give you information because He trusts you.

Take a moment right now and repent if you are in sin and condemnation. Turn away from that sin that is contaminating you and allow Jesus to start using you. Jesus wants to use you. If he can use a donkey, for goodness' sake, he can use you. It is not that He is expecting perfect people, but more so He is expecting people to turn from sin. If you don't know already, Jesus loves you, so can turn from your sin. You can say Jesus come be my friend and help me.

In the book of Acts 10-9-16, it says that about noon the following day as they were on their journey and approaching the city, Peter went up on the roof to pray. He became hungry and wanted something to eat, and while the meal was being prepared, he fell into a trance. He saw heaven opened and something like a large sheet being let down to earth by its four corners. It contained all kinds of four-footed animals, as well as reptiles and birds. Then a voice told him, "Get up, Peter. Kill and eat." "Surely not, Lord!" Peter replied. "I have never eaten anything impure or unclean." The voice spoke to him a second time, "Do not call anything impure that God has made clean." This happened three times, and immediately the sheet was taken back to heaven.

Today, if you tell people that you fell into a trance, they are going to curse you out and throw you out. This is how some church folks are these days. People will think you are doing some weird stuff. I'm here to tell you, based on scripture, that Christians can go into trances. It is mentioned right in the Bible. Yes, people can fall into a trance during prayer and the Lord can reveal Himself. To be in a trance means to be in a sleeplike or half-conscious state. Consciousness is the state of being aware or having knowledge of something. The Lord uses these experiences to reveal His plans to man. Peter saw the sky open and something like a large sheet was let down by its four corners revealing all sorts of animals, reptiles, and birds. Then a voice said to him, "Get up Peter, kill and eat them". "No more", Peter declared, "I have ever eaten anything that our Jewish laws have declared unclean". But the voice spoke again and said, "Do not call something unclean if God has made it clean". I love that that same vision was repeated three times which reveals the significance of Jesus. Let's look at the prophetic meaning behind something being stated three times. For example, Jesus was denied three times. Jesus asked Peter to feed his sheep three times. Also, three times He asked Peter did he love him. Now, he is talking to Peter again, and division is happening three times. He kept hitting Peter with threes. I think it is so wonderful. The sheet was suddenly pulled up to heaven. I think it is awesome that Jesus speaks to us which brings me to something else. If I tell a group of people to close their eyes right now and imagine a pink elephant, all of them are going imagine a pink elephant. But watch this, the pink elephant is going to look different to each person. Some will imagine a skinny pink elephant, while others a big bold pink elephant. Some might even see Dumbo flying around. God speaks to us the way that

He needs to. The voice of the Lord might sound different to you than it does to somebody else. When God uses our imagination, He is going to speak in a way that makes sense to you. So, you must pay attention to your imagination. I'll give you an example. When I see in the spirit, sometimes I see visions of body parts, of a spine, and knees. As I begin praying, healing happens and that confirms that Jesus is the one showing me the body parts in the spirit.

It says in the word of God that signs and wonders follow those who believe. I challenge you to pay close attention to your imagination today. Right now, ask the Lord to show you something about somebody in my life and allow you to see it. Once you do that, you must pay attention to the imagination. Without fail, some people will say this prayer and say to themselves, I can't see anything. Yet, they go throughout their day seeing pictures of what they need to do. They have memories of things that happened to them, but they can't see where the Lord is taking them. What that means is that you have not repented or accepted that you are worthy. Let me inform you now that you are worthy. When you think you are worthy, then you can receive what Jesus has for you. So, your imagination is very important along with the way you feel about yourself. Jesus said this, love the Lord your God with all your strength, mind, and soul. He also said to love your neighbor as yourself. You must receive the love of God in order to give the love of God. If you are going to share a proper vision of what God is showing you, you will need to love the Lord, then love you. It is ok to love you. You should love everything God has created. Love your flaws and all because God uses it for His glory. Amen. Once you do that, you can love the person in front of you appropriately. You will no longer be consumed with self as that is pride and God resists pride because it puts the focus on you. Thus, your imagination is going to be placed on what is wrong with you instead of what God has for somebody else. Today, let's not focus on our faults and shortcomings. Do not focus on comparisons; what is ugly about us and stuff like that. You will not be able to look at someone with the intention of loving them and having an imagery from the Lord while at the same time be focused on you. Repent in your heart and accept that you are worthy.

Some of you will read this book, meditate on the things of God, and receive freedom. Some of you will literally get set free from a spirit of divination. You will be set free from a spirit that has been deceiving and talking to you. You will discover that some things will have come through looking at something wrong or evil. It might have come through a voice, a generational curse that has followed the family or witchcraft that has been blocking you. These spirits may have even lied to you and made you believe that you cannot receive what God has for you, but the truth is you will receive it. We should receive everything that God has for us because He finished the work, he defeated the devil. He crushed his head and He said now I'm the winner and now my children will be winners too. Amen.

When I look at a person and I want to see for them, I'll make sure I am all the way open to receive. In other words, my whole intent is what God is about to say and what He is about to do. When I'm about to minister, my intentions are totally not on myself. I'm doing my best not to have any focus on me but instead on what Jesus wants to do. It is not about me; it is about Him and what He wants to do. If we're about our father's business, we are going to do what your father tells us to do. Some of us today need to become about our father's business. Our father's business is what is most important. So, when I'm about to function in that seer ability, I make sure I'm intentional when I'm looking at somebody. Also, watch this, you must know by faith. You must take the step of faith which will cause the thing that you are hoping for to manifest.

There are times when I have prayed for people that I literally see the demon behind them. I see what it looks like. I even see what it is acting like at times. Sometimes I will look past the person and say give me a second. I'm not going speak to you right now because I see something going on. When I say this, I'll let them know that I'm not talking to them, I'm talking to what is behind you. I'll then say, hey you behind that person, I see what you are doing. Sometimes when I'm praying with someone, for example, someone dealing with a Jezebel spirit. I'll see Jezebel dancing in a red dress be-hind the person. She will start to mock me. There's been times I will say I caught you, you little red dress witch, you got to come out of that person right now. The person would then scream intensely and hit the ground and that demon would ask how did you see me? You are not supposed to see me. How do you know I'm here? I'll say because I got eyes to see what the spirit of the Lord sees. I remember one time a woman brought her husband up front because she wanted him set free. I looked over to the side and saw by the spirit that there was a gargoyle spirit over her. The gargoyle spirit was representing something occultic. I looked at her and I said, you little gargoyle spirit, get off her now. She smacked the ground and started screaming. This describes how the seer anointing functions. You must be available so that the Lord can speak to you, and you'll see things like this. One time I was praying for a girl, and I saw the popular picture of Jesus hiding a big teddy bear behind his back and I asked the girl if she remembered that picture and it touched her heart. She was like I think about that often. Why we would God show me that picture? He did it to affirm her by letting her know that He has a bigger gift for her. God will also use things you have seen through your life to display an image to somebody else that they have seen as well. This is to affirm them and to show that He is a good father.

I'm always available to see. How do I see? I see in the imagination. I see the picture internally. Sometimes I'll see externally. Sometimes I've seen straight up manifestations. Sometimes I've seen things and was like what was that? The Lord has opened my eyes and given me open visions for me to see what is happening in this spirit regarding what is going on in the physical. These things happen sometimes but you must be open and available. Some people will think that they need to go on a fast and pray right now. Well, no not necessarily, just accept it. What did Jesus say? Only believe. It is the mustard seed of faith that will move a mountain. He didn't say go fast to open your eyes. He said only believe because if we tell you to do all these things now, it is putting it back in your ball court. Now you are going into works. I'm not teaching a works doctrine. I teach an "it is finished" gospel. I teach the full gospel. I teach that Jesus finished it all and it is available if you want it. Jesus literally said to them only believe. Today, only believe. Don't go straight into I got to go do something. No, you don't have to go do anything, only believe.

HOW TO USE FAITH

Hebrews 11:1 says, "Now faith is the substance of things hoped for, the evidence of things not seen". When we accept Jesus as savior, the only reason we really come to Him is because we need a hope. We need a blessed assurance. We need salvation. Jesus has given us all of that; however, the way we get that through hope. Once we do that it allows us to receive that free gift by faith, which is the substance of something we are hoping for and evidence that it may not be seen right now. So, Jesus is our hope of salvation. We put our hope and our trust in Him as He is our guarantee that the thing that we hope for is going to manifest in Christ. It takes faith to believe in Jesus Christ. It takes faith to believe in the Gospel. It takes faith to believe in the Bible. Faith is the currency of heaven. Hebrews 11:6 says the only way to even please God is by faith. Unbelief is not even recognized by God, and it is not recognized in His Kingdom either. Faith is very important to the Lord. Abraham was the father of faith; therefore, when you look at other great men and women in the Bible, names like Moses, Joshua, and even Caleb comes to mind when they were looking into the promised land. You also have names like Elijah, Elisha, King David, and Solomon. All these are great names of old but then you have great names today. You see men and women of God were moving in great faith and great power. And it all comes from that simple belief that God is who He says He is, and He will do what He says He will do. So, it takes faith. To believe the same way, faith is the access point of God's power. If you have faith to believe for anything, God's power will be manifesting the thing you are believing for to manifest. Faith is so important. Just now, while you are reading this book, you are believing that God is going to do something in your life. You are believing that there is going to be a manifestation of His goodness in your life, in other words, if you need healing, you are believing by faith that your healing is going to manifest. You might be believing by faith that the demonic torment that has been upon you is going to exit your life. Now listen, I can do demonstrations of faith. Demonstrations of faith is simply demonstrating the power of God. If you line up with what I'm teaching you, by faith, through the word of God, you will see the promises that He has for your life. He can manifest change into your life today. What if I declare that everybody reading this book is going to receive their healing right now? If you believe that 100%, without any doubt in your heart, then you can receive your healing. The Bible says a double minded man is unstable in all his ways. How can he expect to receive anything from God? If you come in unwavering faith, what do you think is going to happen? The manifestation of which you came for is going to happen. The very thing you are asking for is going to come to past. You will see a manifestation of God's power. It even reads in Romans 8:19 that all creation is groaning for the revealing of the sons of God. We, as sons and daughters of

God are going to manifest because creation is begging for us to come into being. Creation is saying I really, really need the sons and daughters to come on the scene. We need somebody that is going to worship the creator of the whole world. Creation is saying we need those men and women who are going to worship the one who created us. Individuals that are going to show us heaven here on earth. You know, Jesus said on "let thy will be done on earth as it is in heaven", thus, our job is to present the manifestation of God's glory here on this earth. God's glorious manifested is shown through us. His glory is also seen throughout all creation. How do we allow people to see God's glory in all creation? We need to make them aware of the creator. Jesus is the word of God, and everything manifested when God spoke words. Jesus is the word that created everything. It reads in Colossians 1:17, that everything is held together through Him and in Him. So, Jesus is the way. Faith also takes risks. Faith costs your unbelief, meaning faith will not allow you to unbelieve. If the Bible says that if you lay hands on the sick, they will recover, that means when you go lay hands on them, you must believe that the sick will recover. Well, some people would say, well Daniel, I pray for people and the healing does not manifest every time. Guess what? There is unbelief right there. Every prayer counts; therefore, when I lay hands, I tell people that I'm believing that you are going to see a manifestation of God's power. In some way because I did my part in faith, I become a conduit of God's power and that manifests His glory and goodness into their life. It is a promise. God's promises are yes and amen. All we have to do is believe what Jesus said in the Bible. He said only believe, that's all you have to do. In Matthew 17:20, it says that if you have faith as a grain of a mustard seed, you can say to this mountain move and it will move. I do not know who is going to read this book nor what type of challenges each reader is facing. But I do believe this, if you take what I am teaching you and apply it to your circumstances, not allowing your challenges to dictate your life anymore, you will see the manifestations of God's power in your life. No longer accept that pain you are feeling in your body. No longer get used to the things that you have been used to in life. Right now, be willing to let the Lord change you. I will make you a Holy Ghost guarantee. I guarantee you will change for the glory of God. Your faith will be honored by Jesus Christ because you believed on him. You took His word at face value. You didn't go ahead and move all over the place and go, well, you know. But maybe not today. Some people will tell themselves that the healings will manifest later. My question to you is why would you accept it later when he said it could be done now? Don't wait till later to receive your blessing. Received blessing and walk right now. Jesus healed 10 lepers. He told them walk and as they walked, they will be be healed. Guess what? They started walking and they were healed. He gave them an instruction and by faith they were able to walk in obedience. That is how this works. If read about Elijah, he threw his cloak on the water. Moses parting the Red Sea. Joshua and Caleb going into the land of the Giants and taking it over. I mean everything looks so big to a lot of people, but when you have a man or woman of faith, what happens? The impossible becomes possible. Great things start to manifest. The goodness of God in our lives, and in this earth, starts to show because of our willingness to believe. Today, I don't know what you are looking for in life. I don't know where your heart is right now. If you are reading this book in faith, you are using the currency of heaven and God is going to give you a return on that deposit. Faith is a deposit because you are depositing something into heaven, and it has a return. The return is your healing. The return is your deliverance. The returning is your salvation and baptism of the Holy Ghost and fire. So, that is you are going to be your return. Say out loud, "God, you said in your word I will be healed. God, you said in your word that I can receive a miracle. God, you said in your word that I can have breakthrough from demonic bondage". If you will hold onto faith that God is going to honor what you said out loud, then he is going to meet you in a big way. As you are reading this book, the words written on each page carries the anointing of God. The Lord has chosen me, and I am a vessel for His Glory. We are vessels for His glory and He no respecter of persons. If you look at me as a man who has been chosen by the Lord Jesus Christ, my words carry weight into your life. If I am hearing from the Lord, the words I release will come into effect in your life. If I declare something is going to happen in your life. Can you believe that? What do you think is going to happen? Healing is going to manifest. If I say you will get delivered, what do you think is going to happen? You are going to get delivered. So, guess what? I'm going to make a Holy Ghost guarantee again. Listen to me, in the name of Jesus Christ of Nazareth. Everybody reading this book right now you will be healed. You will in the name of Jesus Christ of Nazareth be delivered. You will be saved. You will be filled with his Holy Spirit. You will listen again, see the manifestation of His promises in your life.

I titled this chapter how to use faith. Here it is...Believe, believe, believe, only believe and you will see the manifestation of what you are believing. I'm telling you that's how you use faith. That's how you get the pleasing aroma of Jesus in your life. You start to see the manifestation of His goodness. You just believe, even if you are standing in front of a crazy situation in your life right now. You are battling the and addiction. You are battling your spouse. You are battling your friends. You are battling family members. Whatever it may be, if you will only believe, that's all you must do. God is a God that he shall not lie. He is faithful to complete the work that he started in you. If you only believe His promises, you will see the breakthrough that you've been looking for in your life. You will not have to go in your prayer closet and pray 1000 hours again for one promise. All you must do is believe in the promise. I believe a lot of times people are running into their prayer closet or running to various places praying for the same thing over and over and over again. God is simply saying stop having unbelief and just believe that I am a faithful steward of my own word and that I will do what my works says I will do. If some of us would just believe that, then you will see that. Sometimes we get into a works mentalities thinking that God is pleased with our works. He loves the joy we have in the works. He does not love the work we have in the works. You must realize Jesus is our rest. Somebody asked me once "Daniel, what day is the Sabbath?" I replied that if you look at Jewish customs and biblical history, Saturday is the actual Sabbath day. I'm not going to get into legalistic beliefs because I believe every day is the Sabbath. The scriptures say in Matthew 11:28 that if I come to him and I'm tired, he will give me rest. I view Jesus as my Sabbath. This is no offense to any Seventh Day Adventist who might be reading this book; however, the Lord might be using this teaching to deliver you from legalistic religion. Please believe me when I say that Jesus is rest. Jesus is the Sabbath. Jesus is our peace. Jesus is just everything we need; therefore, if you want a Sabbath rest, rest in Christ and you can have all the rest you need. Jesus is the Lord of the Sabbath and the encapsulation of it all. Jesus really made it easy for us.

There is point in scripture where Paul had to rebuke Peter. Why do you think he did that? I believe Peter thought that he could bring circumcision back into the church. Paul said hold on buddy as it is no longer the circumcision of flesh that makes us righteous, just the circumcision of heart. What do you think you are doing by trying to put these people under bondage? So, Paul rebuked Peter because they were getting into a legalistic way or works mentalities. For some of you reading this book, what happens is you get free and then you go looking for the next study you can get into that you feel will bring you deeper revelation. I am going to reveal something to every person reading this book, legalistic and works based teachings can lead you into a wild goose chase which can actually cause you to develop religious beliefs. You know there are people out there that believe if they line everything up correctly based on scripture and current events that they can tell the exact day Jesus will return. This is not true at all. I believe that is a demonic inspiration. The Bible says in Mark 13:32 that no man knows the day or hour, not even the angels in heaven, nor the Son, but only the father when the appointed time will come. Nobody knows, not even Jesus himself when he will return, only His father in heaven knows. He is going to come back in a physical form and will put his rod and scepter down to rule and to reign as King. We must remove some of the legalistic ways that we adopt that brings unbelief into our lives. We need to focus on winning souls. Keep the gospel simple and don't over consume yourself with things that you can't change or do anything about. Some people really get fed on trying to search out and seek these things. I used to be one of the people. It is not worth it guys. It is not worth it. Don't go down rabbit holes and stay in a place of just believing the impossible. Going out there, see the Kingdom come and His will be done in the earth. I want to instill in the body of Christ how to keep things simple and not to get overwhelmed with religiosity and a lot of works. I live so free and simple. I have a great life of Jesus. And of course, like most people, I go through persecutions from time to time. In my refining moments, where I'm in the refiner's fire, God changes things in my life making me better for his glory.

How does a person inherit the Kingdom of God? You must become like a child. Children have a lot of faith. Children are not contaminated. It is until we get older, and information starts coming into our ears and eyes that starts to mess us up. Once that happens, we start to lose faith. For all my readers, I am praying this today that you will come back to that childlike faith. Some people may be saying right now, "Well, you do not understand my childhood. I never got to be a child". You know what? When you are born again, that childhood is passed away. In 2 Corinthians 5:17, it says that there if anyone is in Christ, he is a new creation. The old things have passed away and behold, the new has come. So, let it just go. Let the past go. I know some of us had childhoods where we went through really bad stuff, but let it go. Allow God to help you develop the childlike faith that he has always wanted you to have. We die with Christ; we rise with Christ. We are rising as a new creation. Right where you, say out loud "I am new creation in Christ Jesus". We are a new creation. We are sons and daughters. We are ambassadors and have a divine inheritance from the Kingdom of God.

HOW TO HEAR GOD'S VOICE

Everybody wants to know how to hear God's voice. One of the most common questions I am asked is "How can I hear God's voice or what I am doing to not be able to hear God's voice?" When it comes to hearing God's voice, it is very simple. First, it is important to be saved; however, you do not have to be saved to hear His voice. His voice has chased many of us down even when we were unbelievers. When you are an unbeliever, he's speaking in different ways to get your attention. You know the Lord is always speaking, if you have eyes to see and ears hear you'll see God speaking through everything. You will be able to prophetically pick things up all over the place. Secondly, you must know His word. You must listen for His voice through His word. Again, even unbelievers are being chased down by God's voice. As a result, you get saved by that voice, whether is comes through a person, through a divine encounter, through a dream or open vision. Many have heard the voice of God by watching a sermon. There are many ways God's voice can chase you down. When His voice chases you down and you surrender to it by saying "Yes" in your heart to His salvation, you become saved.

Now, as a child of God, you have a responsibility of learning what His voice sounds like, and that comes after salvation. Again, God is always speaking. He is speaking through all of creation. He speaks through the elements, like the rain and wind. God speaks in ways that would blow our mind. Elijah ran in a cave in fear of Jezebel taking his life. The bible says it rained, there was an earthquake, and thunder but it was in a still small voice that God spoke. Elijah must have been aware of how God speaks that he was able to discern His voice.

Let us now go back to the very beginning of time. God has been with mankind from the moment Adam and Eve came on the scene in the Garden of Eden. In Genesis 3:8 it says that Adam and Eve heard the sound of the Lord God walking in the garden in the cool of the day and among the trees of the garden. The man and his wife hid themselves from the presence of the Lord God among the trees of the garden. So, even from the beginning, Adam and Eve knew God's voice and presence. They were aware of His existence and knew when he showed up. Can you imagine, God just walking by and witnessing the trees and the elements moving in response to His presence? This was Adam and Eve's reality until sin came on the scene. We are going to discuss this more later in the chapter because it is one of the main causes that prevent you from hearing God's voice.

Jeremiah 33:3 says, "Call to me and I will answer you and will tell you great and hidden things that you have not known". This scripture reveals a God that desires relationship. It is God saying "Hey, talk to me and I'll show you somethings. Lock yourself away, speak to me and I'll answer you". Romans 10:17 says "Faith comes from hearing and hearing through the word of Christ". One of the first ways to hear God's voice is through His word. I'll tell you this, if you don't know His word, Jesus, the written word of God, the word made flesh, then you will be led astray by the thoughts, emotions and words that come into your mind. In other words, you will be in trouble. The bible says that His sheep knows His voice and a stranger they will not follow. In John 8:47 it says, "Whoever is of God, hears the word of God". Another reason why you may not be able to hear His voice is because you are not of God. So, whoever is of God, hears the words of God. Again, in John 10:27 it says, "My sheep hear my voice and I know them, and they follow me". Also, they will not listen to the voice of another man.

There are many scriptures on hearing the voice of God. Please understand that knowing His word is the first step in knowing His voice. So, if a voice comes to you and says go jump off that bridge. Is that the voice is God? Obviously not. But if you are walking in public and notice someone and begin to have a strong feeling to talk to them, that is more than likely the Lord's voice unctioning you by His Spirit. You might not hear an audible voice, but just a knowing on the inside of you that you need to talk to that person. In essence, that is the Lord's voice pushing you gently to speak to that person and share the good news. You might also hear in your heart a word of knowledge through the voice of God. The Lord can reveal to you that the person had a car accident, and their back is injured. Sadly, what happens is the voice of doubt comes in, through being so self-aware, which results in many missing opportunities with the Holy

Spirit. Unfortunately, oftentimes, as soon as you hear the voice of God, the voice of doubt, the enemy, will come back behind what God has said whispering lies. The next thing you know, you are questioning if what you heard was God from the beginning. The devil will ask you things like what if that person gets offended? What if they don't like you and get angry? Or he'll even tell you that maybe it is not the right time for them to hear the good news. You see, that is the voice of the enemy.

Faith is the substance of things hoped for, the evidence of things not seen. I'll tell you this, if what you heard requires faith, it is God's voice. However, if it causes you to back up and not step out in faith, it is probably the voice of the enemy trying to keep you from glorifying Jesus Christ in your life. I mean, there's not a man or woman in the world that does not suffer with the temptation to not pursuit what God has spoken. You know, the fear of man is a snare. It is a snare to those who are trying to pursue the things of God because we become so concerned with what the other person thinks or what the repercussions would be. So, we ask questions like, should I say this? What's going to happen if I do this? These kinds of questions come is really one of the things that stifles us frequently as the body of Christ. When God's voice is speaking to you, it will always require risk. It will always require you to step out and do something that will make you look crazy and probably bring you persecution for righteousness's sake. You know people will ask why is he doing that? Or, they'll say that this makes no sense. The next thing you know, during the persecution, the miracle comes. When the miracle comes, they say, wow, that person knows God. It is just like when we prophesy, we do it by faith. God's voice requires faith, and it can sound like so many things. It can sound like yourself when God speaks to you just so that His words reach you.

Again, God can speak in a way where it sounds like your voice, but it is important to note that you will never know if you do not go. You will walk around in circles. You will traverse that mountain until you step out and go, and then you'll be able to identify, oh, that's God's voice. And then you will become aware of His voice. You know we look at great men and women of God are amazed because they do it with such ease. They make it look easy, but the reason they make it look easy is because they know what His voice sounds like. They have become accustomed to hearing it. When you think of babies, when the parent comes in the room, the baby knows it because it knows their voice. The baby knows that they know the voice of the mother and father. They become attentive to the voice. It is the same way with us being children of God, we become attentive. You know we give our attention to the voice that we know. On the other hand, many of us know the voice of the enemy way more and we give our attention to him. Thus, by giving our attention to the enemy, we get the results of listening to that voice. But Jesus says, my sheep hear my voice and another they will not follow. All throughout the bible you can read about men and women of God being able to hear God's voice. Take a man like Moses who went up on the mountain where there were clouds all around. I mean some crazy activities were going on. One can only imagine the way that they were hearing God's voice during the Old Covenant and the faith they had to have to perceive it. I'm telling you God is speaking on a consistent basis.

One day I was in the gym and heard a voice. I heard the voice say "Daniel, do a TikTok today on depression and pray for the people who are suffering from it". I went and did what the voice said, and I had great results because of it. I had great results because of listening to the still, small voice, or internal unctioning of God. It sounds like a thought, or inner conversation. What is the mystery revealed? It is Christ in you, the hope of Glory. Where does the spirit of God reside? The answer is in you. It says the Christ in you, and it says that the same spirit that raised Christ from the dead resides in you. I want to make sure you guys have an understanding and awareness of God's voice in a way you did not before. So, knowing God's word, you'll understand the internal unctionings. Mark 16:15-18 is about the Great Commission. If God says lay hands on somebody and they'll be healed, guess what? You got to go heal the sick. If He says that a particular person has a demon and cast it out, guess what's going to happen? You are going to have a result. If it is God's voice you will have a "God result".

Let's talk about speaking in unknown tongues. Carnality can get in the way of us hearing God. So, when we pray in the spirit, unknown tongues, it strengthens us. It aligns us to God and shifts our focus on Him. Because once we're calibrated and focused, now the voice of God becomes quite apparent to us. Also, praying in the spirit moves your attention away from the world. His spirit is interceding through you. Knowing God's word and paying attention to the internal unctions is vital. Walking with the Lord daily, the same way Adam and Eve walked in the garden of Eden. Let me tell you something, you are doing that now if you are believer in Jesus Christ. You are born again. You are filled with the Holy Spirit; therefore, Eden is within you now. Know you were walking in the promise of God. You are walking in the inheritance. You just have to realize it. You are not meant to be known in this world. You are not meant to be like some of these famous celebrities. You goal is make Jesus famous. Our job here on earth as men and women of God, who are growing in the same gift, is to make Jesus famous. How do we make Jesus famous? We know our father's voice and by knowing our father's voice we are able to exalt His son in this earth through His Holy Spirit. Now, the only way you can achieve this is by listening to His voice.

Hearing God's voice is so simple. You can even practice hearing His voice after reading this book. If you sit down and grab a journal, get quiet, and internally listen to what is going on. Listen to your thoughts. Dialogue with God and then become aware of how He wants to speak. You know He can speak in anyway. God can speak through a message. Right now, he's speaking to you through this book as I believe these words are divinely inspired by the Holy Ghost. God can speak through different things. Most importantly, God wants to be able to speak internally to you because He is living on the inside of you. So, take a seat, grab a pen and journal. Now, simply ask the Lord to speak to you. Once you've done that, just be quiet and listen. You might hear God say, "I want to bless you so that you can go feed the homeless tomorrow". Some of you will question is because it sounds too vague and simple to you. Some of you will doubt the word thinking that God speaks in a much bigger way. Here is another example, you may hear God say, "I want you to call your parents and ask them for forgiveness for the way things were when you were younger". Many of you will doubt these words but I'm here to tell you that both are God's voice. This is how God speaks. Why? Because it is going to cause His Kingdom to manifest on Earth is going to be. It is going to make people aware of his Kingdom. So, when find a quiet moment, sit down, grab a journal, and write. Journaling is great for people that are trying to hear and learn God's voice.

Trust what you are hearing on the inside and then practice. The Lord may ask you to speak to your friends about Him. Write it all down in the journal and then call your friends and say, hey I am practicing hearing the Lord and I believe He told me to tell you something. Now, it is important to be careful saying that the Lord said this, and the Lord said that, unless you are absolutely confident. If you are accurate, your friend will confirm the word or tell you to keep practicing. Ultimately, practicing with family and friends is a great way to know if you are hearing God's voice accurately. As you continue practicing, you will begin finding yourself operating in prophesy, words of knowledge, discernment, revelatory gifts, and wisdom. You will start to become more confident and aware of God's voice.

Do you understand God is talking to you? I promise He is talking to you 24/7. All you got to do is become aware. There are so many things in the world that pursues our attention. If we can only place our attention on Him. Once we do that, all we must do is trust that He's talking to us. In the beginning of my journey of hearing God's voice, I was a little uncertain but as I practiced and learned through spending time with Him and reading his word, I am confident in knowing His voice.

Now, let's delve into the types of things that can prevent you from hearing God's voice. First, you will not be able to hear God's voice if you are in willing sin. Now, you may hear Him at times try to get your attention so that you can tun away from sin, but if you have unconfessed sin in your life, it will block your ability to hear. When you are in willing sin, demonic voices are going to overpower God's voice. I mean they going to just try their best to make sure you don't hear God's voice which will lead you in a path of destruction. This ultimately the enemy's job which is to steal, kill and destroy. Jesus said my sheep know my voice and a stranger they will not follow. So, the enemy's voice will lead you to destruction every time. Sin is a sure way to miss God's voice. I mean as a non-believer, being in sin, consciously aware and knowing that you are doing it. Essentially, you are going to struggle to hear God's voice because you have placed your attention on your flesh and the things of this world.

Let's talk about unconfessed sin. What does the bible say about it? It says that everything done in the dark will be revealed in the light. You must confess everything. God voice will speak to you louder than ever before the moment all the shame is gone. What is what does the Bible say? There is no guilt, shame, or condemnation in Christ Jesus. If you are living outside of the promises, and the reality of what Christ has done for you, you are going notice all types of issues in your life. Some will notice poverty, no abundance, and rebellion to name a few. You know Bible says rebellion is as the sin of witchcraft. Witchcraft is the opposite of the blessing. It attacks, devours, blocks you from being able to move forward in life. Overall, you are not able to break past these barriers. You are also not able to see the things about your life because you have that unconfessed sin. One of the first things you need to do coming into Christ is to bare it all. I mean lay it completely out there before the Lord. I don't care how nasty it is. I personally have sat in front of people who confessed to killing someone and many other really bad things. Now, I'm not talking about someone struggling through something and breaking through on the other side because that is God's voice leading you out. I'm talking about the things that you think nobody knows about and you think the Lord doesn't see. What did Adam and Eve do? They tried to hide. Listen, God knows everything and there's nothing hidden from Him that he is unable to see. He knows everything we think about and do in the dark. His eyes are everywhere, all the time. He's omniscient, omnip-otent, and omnipresent. He is the great I Am. What did Je-sus just say? I AM. "I Am" is the in capsulation of all that God is.

In Romans 8:7 says, "Because the carnal mind is enmity against God: for it is not subject to the law of God, neither indeed can be". In I Thessalonians 5:19 says, "Do not stifle or quench the Holy Spirit". Carnal is what we were before we came into Christ. Now we're renewed in the Spirit and born again. We are a new creation in Christ Jesus; there-fore, the carnal mind must die as we put the mind of Christ. When you operate in the carnal nature or mindset, accord-ing to Galatians 5, you operate in works of the flesh which prevents you from inheriting the Kingdom of God. You can-not operate in the works of the flesh and be able to walk in the fruits of the spirit at the same time. You must be able to walk in the fruits of the spirit to hear the voice of God. Again, when you walk in the flesh, you walk in the things of the carnal nature which results in not being able to inherit the Kingdom of God. You cannot inherit the Kingdom of God walking in carnality. So, just because you are operating in a gifting does not mean God's voice is always speaking. A gifting does not verify that you are really hearing the au-thentic voice of God. When the authentic voice of God is manifest in a person's life, you will see amazing miracles, signs, wonders, and breakthrough. You will see abundance, growth and things start to happen because that person is tuned into heaven. I'm not talking about being persecuted, locked up in jail for preaching the gospel. I am not talking about that type of persecution. Paul said in Philippians 4:12-13 that "I know both how to have a little, and I know how to have a lot. In all circumstances I have learned the secret of being content – whether well fed or of going hungry, of having plenty and of being in need. I can do all things through Him who strengths me". I am talking about when you are doing the Kingdom, God is supplying. When you are doing the Kingdom, God is backing you up and sending you places. When you hear God's voice, nothing can stop you. No angel, demon or anything can separate you from the love of God. Do hear the truth I'm speaking? This is the truth. But the carnal nature, the flesh nature of man takes you away from hearing God's voice. This is why the unbeliever looks at some of us like we are crazy; however, when the Lord speaks through us, the unbeliever hits the ground and glorifies the Lord. In I Corinthian 14:24-25 But if all of you are prophesying, and unbelievers or people who don't understand these things come into your meeting, they will be convicted of their sin and judged by what you say. As they listen, their secret thoughts will be exposed, and they will fall to their knees and worship God, declaring, "God is truly here among you".

So, put away the carnal nature. You are not a doubter anymore; you are a believer. You don't have to doubt yourself. Don't be in self-pity either saying "Oh poor me, I'm different. God does not hear me. I have this problem and that problem". What you do not understand is that heart posture is pride. Self-pity is a symptom of pride. This is another factor that is going to block your ability to hear the

Lord. What does it say in the word of God? In 1 Peter 5:5 "God resists the proud but gives grace to the humble". Even in the old covenant, Job 41:15 it references of the scales of his pride being sealed tightly together that nothing can penetrate it. In other words, the Holy Spirit cannot speak to someone that is full of pride. It is impossible. Making statements "Oh, woah is me. I can't get free. I can't repent". Those types of statements are form of manipulation. You might not even know you are doing it because you grew up being exposed to it. Unfortunately, it is pride, and it will prevent you from hearing the voice of God because it shifts the focus to self. Oftentimes, people who battle depression, do not realize that demonic spirits leverage a person overly consumed by self. Again, it is quite impossible for the voice of the Holy Spirit to breakthrough unless you come to realization that things have been made to be all about you. So, how can I possibly hear the voice of the Holy Spirit for somebody else if the focus is on what I must do and what I need. Avoid self-pity. Please know that everyone reading this book right now is capable of hearing the Holy Spirit. God is not a respecter of persons. All you have to do is repent and turn your heart to His voice and believe. Jesus said the faith of a mustard seed will move a mountain. He said the only believe and you can receive. John 14:14 says "You may ask anything in my name, and I will do it". Romans 12:2 talks about being transformed by the renewing of your mind that by testing you may discern what is the will of God, what is good, acceptable, and perfect.

You will know what God's will is for your life. Many times, people come to me and ask "Daniel, what is God's will for my life?" I say to them you should know God's will. You should really go seek Him in your prayer closet because when you sit with Him for a little bit, you are going to know exactly what God has told you to do. You will go after your passions and desires. Sometimes, I'll even sit with people and help them. That is what the gifts of Holy Spirit are for; therefore, I will prophesy to them and bring word of knowledge that confirms what God has called them to do in life. Praise God for the gifts of the Holy Spirit because it can be used to breakdown walls and barriers in a person's life so that they can walk into their call. What is important is although God can use me to speak into someone's life, that person but not be led to look at me as their prophetic mouthpiece for hearing God. That is old covenant. We should all know God's voice; therefore, you must go to the prayer closet for yourself. I do not want to be anyone's savior but instead, I want to lead you to the savior. This is significance of the 5-Fold ministry which is to lead people to hearing God's voice.

So, ask yourself right now, what is the biggest thing blocking you from hearing God's voice? I can tell you it is sin. Oftentimes, it is hidden secrets, those things you do not think is really affecting you. Yeah, any sin is going to nullify God's voice to an extent. Just know if a voice speaks like the devil, it is the devil. If it speaks like God, it is God and it is that simple. It is so simple. Once you really grasp this revelation, you will never want to go back to listening to the enemy's voice. I know sometimes it is feels like the whole world is caving in on you, but it is in those moments that we can praise God. According to Matthew 15:13, he gives a garment of praise for the spirit of heaviness. Praise him and watch what happens. All those things will go away because the enemy cannot be around praise. When David was going through some of the biggest struggles of his life, like committing murder and adultery, what did he do? He kept praising. He kept saying, Lord, you are my deliverer. B Lord, you are my healer. Bless the Lord, oh my soul, and all that is within me. God deserves all the glory even in the midst of calamity. You must ensure He gets the glory because I'm telling you, it is so easy to get wrapped up in self. Once you begin operating out of self-pity, you are not going to hear the voice of God.

The truth is the devil wants you to believe that he doesn't exist. I'm going to be real with you. He doesn't want you to believe that is he is not lurking around trying to get involved in your affairs. This is so you cannot see his actions at work so that you can put your focus on self. What is the sin that got Satan kicked out of heaven? Pride. The worship of self. Guess what he wants us to do? He wants us to worship ourselves as well. If you can get you to become prideful, he doesn't need to infest you with demons, put witchcraft attacks on you. He knows pride will result in your destruction. Your demise is his ultimate goal. He wants you to destroy yourself. He wants to keep you in sin which leads to death. When you are in sin, sickness can come upon your body. When we operate in worry, doubt, and unbelief, our body is not meant to handle that kind of stress. This is why Jesus told us to cast all of our cares upon Him. There is God's voice again. He says cast your cares of me for my yoke is easy and my burden is light. These are all truths that we can walk and live in. Receive this as a prophetic word. Cast your cares upon the Lord and he will give you rest. That is the word of God. People often compliment me about how well the Lord uses me in word of knowledge. Can I tell how I am able to operate in that way? I spend hours upon hours and days fasting and in prayer. I sat with the Lord through the beginning of my walk just seeking His face. I cried and travailed in need of Him. Although, the Lord was with me the whole time, he wanted to get me in a place where I realized my need of Him. At one point in my life, I thought I had it all, and that lead me into a downward spiral. Today, I can hear His voice because of my need of Him which places a desire to constantly seek His.

I created the TSNL Forerunner school to help people learn these simple truths. I mean it is really that simple, but we tend to lean towards making God complicated. Jesus said three words on the cross. He said it is finished. In other words, it is done. Now, we can live in the Gospel of grace. It is the good news of Jesus Christ. You can spread it. He has chosen you by allowing you to be His mouthpiece. Again, everyone reading this book can hear His voice. I'm telling you; you can get so captivated in Christ that in your dreams and as you are going about each day, you can experience His glory and presence. It is really, really awesome to hear the voice of the Holy Spirit. I pray this chapter has encouraged and inspired you to press in to hear God's voice. Again, the key to not hear being able to hear the voice of God is re-maining self-focused. Remaining in sin will hinder your re-lationship with God. Jesus will have a hard time being your friend because you are resisting Him. Essentially, when we continue in sin, we are telling God that His voice is not good enough. Put away sin and watch how God will transform your life.

OVERCOMING OFFENSE

The spirit of offense is a dangerous thing, and we cannot seem to talk about it enough. You can read about it all in the Bible. Anybody who got offended ended up doing something reckless which as a result caused them a lot of problems. Here is the interesting fact, oftentimes, people do not realize they are dealing with the spirit of offense because it is so ingrained into their behavior. Essentially, they are used to being offended. Since I've been in ministry for a I s have witness many Christians dealing this spirit. And you know, we talk about people who get demonized all the time. A demon must be rooted in offense because offense is unforgiveness. Offense is a very dangerous and it is what the devil uses to snare people because it will prevent you from moving forward in the things of God. Offense also makes you become like the devil because he was kicked out of heaven. The devil is probably the most offending creature that exists. So, the devil wants us to be like him. A good example of the fleshly aspect of offences is if someone says something to you, and you feel the need to immediately defend yourself. I'm sure many of us has done that from time to time. But what that response means says is you have eaten the snare of offense like it is a cheerio. In other words, you just opened your mouth and chewed on it, it then becomes sin in your heart, and now the spirit of offense or rejection is coming into your heart. Offense opens the doors for significant troubles to enter your life. Have you noticed how difficult it is to have a conversation with offended people? You cannot have a conversation with them. The reason being is because they are always in a place of defense. But what we must realize is God is our avenger. God is our defender. So, if God is our avenger and defender, why do we have to say anything at all? There is a great book out there called "The Tale of Three Kings". You will learn about the life of David, Saul, and Absalom. When you delve into the lives of these three kings, you will notice Saul was an offended man, Absalom was an offended son, and David was the only one that really gave everything to God.

Offense is a challenging spirit to overcome. I'm not saying it is an overnight thing; however, it can be. A person must be truly ready to surrender everything over to God. Unfortunately, oftentimes offense is something that can be operating within a person for a long time. Remember, I'm talking about Christians; however, if you are not a Christian, the Gospel of Jesus Christ can cause offense to those who are perishing. On the other hand, the Gospel is a life force, it is everything to those who are saved (Romans 17). Proverbs 19:11 says this, "Good sense makes one slow to anger and it is his glory to overlook an offense". It is the glory of God to overlook an offense. Essentially doing such will cause you to win a brother or sister over. You are going to win a family member over. You are going to win somebody over to Jesus Christ when you overlook an offense. So, it is a glorious thing not to become offended. It is a glorious thing to be able to stand there as one who is rooted in Christ and not take the fiery darts of the enemy as offense. He shoots his darts with the goal of causing offense. I am telling you that most demonic entry points are from offense. I just know that it takes an offended person to receive a demon.

Why do Christians have demons? Well, one of the reasons is because they have unforgiveness and offensive in their heart. Offences is unforgiveness and once it is in your heart a person becomes carnal again. Essentially, that person becomes like the world. Jesus said to Peter, noticing that he was in a state of carnality because he wanted to stop the will of God, to get behind me Satan. Peter was speaking in the ways of man, not with the ways of God. We must know the word of God. In Ecclesiastes 7:21-22 says, "Do not take to heart all the things that people say, lest you hear your servant cursing you. Your heart knows that many times you yourself have cursed others". What he is saying is not to entertain gossip. Don't even entertain what someone is saying about you. Don't give room to offense. If someone is talking about you, let them talk. I used to care about what everybody said about me. Overtime, the Lord had to prepare me for the platform I have today because if I was not prepared, I would have failed. Just look at some of the comments people post on my videos. Sometimes people always have something crazy to say to me. If I really cared about those negative comments, I would be one very offended individual. Every now and then I might respond to someone with a religious spirit in order to help them open their eyes. Come to think of it, I am sure Jesus didn't sound too cool even when he confronted the Pharisees calling them a bunch of dead bones with no life inside of them. Imagine if Jesus said that today. Jesus would offend some people but keep in mind, it was offensive that they were displaying His father in the wrong way. Jesus was upset probably thinking how dare you put a heavy yoke on these people that you cannot even sustain yourself. Jesus did not like anyone misrepresenting the father. What does the father represent? He represents love, compassion, mercy, gentleness, kindness, and self-control. All the fruits of the spirit are what the father represented which differed from what the Pharisees represented.

Proverbs 18:19 says this "A brother offended is more unyielding than a strong city, and quarreling is like the bars of a castle". When you offend someone, and that person takes on a spirit of offense, you will more than like not be able to win that person over, unless they forgive you. A person who walks around in offense will not drop that wall. They will not yield and will argue their point. They will make sure that they are understood because they feel misunderstood. We really need to open our heart to this teaching. If you notice that you are in conversations where you are in the defense all the time, there is a root of offense in your heart. Today, you can literally let that go. I mean, literally, at this very moment, you can say to Jesus, I put this offense down. If you been hurt in relationships such as a friendship or even by your own parents, you can literally give it to God and get set free. I have noticed that when people get set free from the spirit of offense, I have seen them get flown back almost every time. It is like the Holy Spirit just pushes that stuff off them because if you are offended, you don't really want to lose dignity. Often when people deal with the offence, you know the Lord deals with them in an amazing way. It is quite cool to see how God touches and loves on them in a special way. Once they are free, they realize they were offended for no reason.

Why do people fall that way when they are getting delivered from the spirit of offense or rejection? Because it is a strong wall. It is a wall and what causes a wall to be knocked down? A force. In other words, the person gets hit by the power of the Holy Ghost. What happens next is that wall of offense comes down. Then the person notices that they did not realize they were holding on to all that offense. The person does not realize it because the wall of offense comes into the heart and germinates through the body, essentially, taking over. When you think of faith, it is like a mustard seed. Faith grows if it is in the right place. But guess what? Sin is the same way; a seed of sin can run right through your body and just tear everything up. What seed do you want growing inside of you? Do you want to take more offense on or more faith?

Today, put your offences down. If someone is near you right now that you need to forgive, this is your chance. Forgive them. I'll give you 100% guarantee that if you will put your walls of offense down, I promise that demon will come off you so fast. That demon will kick rocks and leave town. And if you have never been filled with the Holy Spirit, He will fill you quicker than you can say the word "Holy Spirit". It will hit you so hard and fast that it will rock you. It happens every time someone releases offence. The Holy Ghost goes wow, you are in my character again, because I am a forgiving God, I'm going to come and be a part of what you got going on. Sometimes people tell me that they cannot feel the Holy Ghost. I tell them the reason you cannot feel the Holy Ghost is because you are offended. So, if someone comes to your heart that upset you, just let it go.

A spirit of offense can turn into bitterness. Offense is also the entry point to everything else. Offense can cause the spirit of rejection to attach itself to you. Offense can cause the spirit of pride to attach itself to you. Offense can cause the spirit of anger to attach itself to you as well. The spirit of bitterness can cause Leviathan to eventually enter your life as well. Offense can cause the Jezebel to enter your life. You see how this works? Offense can cause several spirits to enter your life to not only destroy you but to cause you to be unable to not only hear God's voice. The devil needs offense to get into your life. He lives on offense. He lives on a fence. He lives on the in between. That's why Jesus said I'd rather you be hot or cold, not lukewarm. Offense will make you double minded because you really can't sustain yourself with the word of God when you are offended. You will not want to pray because there's another God in your life which is the god of offense. When you have the god of anger there is no way you are going to be able to commune with the Lord when you are not carrying His characteristics.

Now, for a new believer, it takes time. God has grace for them. Allow me to explain. Grace covers what you do not know, but it has a hard time covering what you do know because you are nullifying the power of the blood of Jesus Christ. Now, you are a believer saying His blood is not good enough because I want to hold on to offense. Essentially, what you are literally saying is that the offense is more important than the blood. How can grace possibly cover that? Jesus is grace and truth, in addition, his grace works with truth. Truth causes grace to come into your life. Remember that the enemy wants us to stay in that place of offence so that we block God's grace. However, as soon as we let the wall down, here comes God's grace to cover and empower us to not be offended anymore so that we can walk into where we are called to be.

I literally feel that there are people reading this book who just had an argument with your loved one. You literally just had an argument with your spouse, boyfriend or girlfriend, or friend. Guess what? That is offence folks. All arguments a birth from offence. You are probably thinking, well Daniel, this person did me wrong. My response to you is found again in Ecclesiastes 7:21-22 which basically says to not entertain the wrong done to you. Simply let it go. What happened to Jesus Christ? Jesus had the biggest right to be offended, more than all of us. So many of the ones that followed him which includes the people He delivered, the people He loved on, and the people that He gave arms to are the same ones who put Him on the cross. He could have said I am going to wipe all of you guys off the face of the earth, but he didn't, instead, he said to the father to forgive them. Jesus knew they were acting in a mindset that God never created them to have and didn't realize what they were doing. Again, Jesus told Peter to get behind me, Satan. When Jesus got on the across, you know what he said? He said get behind me Satan. Essentially, what Jesus was saying was get behind me offense. Get behind me rejection. Get behind me pride. Get behind the anger. Get behind me to sin. You know why? Because he was saying I'm yielding the fruit of the spirit and about to pour the Holy Spirit upon all mankind. So, devil, you cannot have my children bound to offense anymore. You can't have the people that I have chosen mad, angry, bitter, sick, and overcome by things any longer. I'm not going to allow that to happen anymore.

Today, you can be set free. Today, the Lord can remove all of that stuff from your life and get you living in His perfect will. Another scripture commonly used in ministry is found in Matthew 18 beginning at verse 15. This passage deals with how to deal with someone that is offended which involves bringing in that person and then additional people if that person will not take down the wall of offense. Pride is a terrible spirit and will keep a person down for a long time. According to Matthew 18, if you have a brother that is offended at your brother or sister in Christ, and they are not receiving what you are saying by taking the forgiveness you are offering, you go grab additional people. If that person still refuses to listen, according to scripture you are to tell it to the church, and if they refuse to listen even to the church, treat them as you would a pagan or tax collector. This obviously is directed to the church, but it works in everyday life as well because our goal is to win all people to Christ.

Many of us have went through traumatic experiences in our life like abuse. In divorce, sometimes children feel abandoned by a parent. These types of traumatic experiences can create roots of offensive in our life that we seldom realize. People look at me at times amazed by how God is using me but what they must realize is that for me to be used mightily by God I must be free. I must be free from offense because there is no way I can love people properly otherwise. I cannot move in the power of the Holy Spirit properly with offense. Here is another truth, if there is offense in your heart, you will begin to doubt yourself making it very difficult to minster deliverance to someone else. You are supposed to bring healing to people with the revelation of you yourself has been healed. You are supposed to bring the deliverer to them with the revelation that you yourself has been delivered. I'll say it again, offense is a dangerous thing. It is the bait of Satan.

You are not a victim if you are a Christian. There are no victims in Christ. and listen. I have probably hundreds of Christians offend at me. Of course, not trying to offend them because they never released offense from their heart. An offended person has a rebellious spirit. They will always work in a witchcraft spirit. If you have a offense in your heart, oftentimes, you will have a witchcraft spirit attached to you because that spirit will tell you lies which causes torment you and deception. If somebody is walking around with offense in their heart, they might be your best friend, or relative, all it takes is you saying one thing wrong, and you have lost them. They will be out of there because of offense. So, if you have daddy issues, you are going to have issues with every person in your life. If you have mommy issues, you are going to have problems with everybody in your life. What does one of the 10 command- ments say about how we should treat our parents? Exo- dus 20:12, "Honor your father and mother, that your days may be long upon the land which the Lod your God is giving you". There is a reason God said obey or honor your parents so that your life will be long. Your parents are usually the people you must start with tearing down offense. Look, I know there are people out there that were abandoned or brutally mistreated by their parents. I am here to tell you that you can get spiritually healed from all of it. You can actually be delivered from everything you went through by the hands of your parents. Again, they are the ones you start with in tearing down offense. Once you have said yes to Jesus, you have no excuses. When you leave this earth and stand before God, are you doing to say daddy did me wrong or mommy did this to me? He is not going to want to hear that because essentially, you were following the wrong Jesus. Do not stand before Jesus as a victim. I want to stand in front of God and hear him Daniel you forgave people, well done good and faithful servant. You understood and won the race. You ran and made it.

Release offense today. You can do it. God made us more than conquerors. We are victorious. So, let down the of- fense and watch your life radically change.

UNDERSTANDING THE ANOINTING

I f you do not know it yet, you are anointed and appointed for something awesome in this life. In Jeremiah 1:5 it says that "before I formed you in the womb I knew you, before you were born, I set you apart, I appointed you as a prophet to the nations". God knew you and predestined you putting something extraordinary upon your life. I don't care what you went through or how many sins you committed in your life. I don't care what nation, city, or town you are from. None of that matters. If you believe in Jesus Christ, you are going to walk into your calling and destiny. You are the handiwork of God as you are fearfully and wonderfully made. He has given you something so special. I believe I am anointed to bring the body of Christ into their callings and destinies. One of my biggest heartbeats is to see Christians become everything they are called to be in Christ which is ultimately to see people walking in power and authority. What is the point in being a Christian if you are going to be religious and boring? God didn't intend for us to be religious and boring Christians. If you notice in scripture, anybody Jesus talked to He gave them power and authority. He even appointed 70 people with power and authority to cast out demons. Jesus gave his disciples power and authority to heal the sick, cast out demons, raised the dead, cleanse the leper saying freely you received, freely give. It is a great commission according to Mark 16:15-18 that is directed to all believers. Guess what? If you are a believer, you have been commissioned, predestine, and anointed by Jesus Christ for a work on this earth. Please know that you are on this earth for His glory and to proclaim His story.

I knew I was anointed before I was anointed if that makes sense. There are people reading this book right now that knew early on in life you were many different. You knew that there as something about you that differed from others. You felt it in your heart that there is something people are not noticing. There something on me that people keep overlooking and neglecting, while on the inside you just want to shout to the world, "Hey, I'm here, God. Let these people see that I'm willing". There is someone reading this book right now that knows they have been called and anointed since you were very young. As long as you can remember, you loved God, and just could not understand why He loved you so much asking yourself what it was about you. You also wondered why you were bullied and picked on. All of it was because the Lord has put something on you. The enemy has known that there is something special on your life so he made sure he threw as much as he could at you to try stop you from knowing you are anointed and appointed. I want everyone reading this book to say out loud right now "I am anointed and appointed. Today is the day that I will catch fire for Jesus Christ". If you said that you just prophesied and publicly declared to the Holy Spirit, and the world that today is your day. So, get ready because that means the Holy Ghost is about to hit you and rock your world.

In Ephesians 2:10, it says, "For we are his workmanship, created in Christ Jesus for good works, which God prepared beforehand, that we should walk in them". Here's the key... for good works which God prepared beforehand that we should walk in them. So, right there you see that God has prepared beforehand good works for you to walk in. He even says you are His handiwork. How amazing is that? I am telling you right now, everyone reading this book, you are created for something special. I don't care if you been diagnosed with a mental disorder. I don't care if you are bi-polar or schizophrenic and feel crazy. I don't care if you feel depressed, or any of those things. Guess what? God can remove all of that and get you into your anointed and appointed call.   Just know that there is nothing you are going through that disqualifies you from your destiny and calling. Actually, there are only two people that can disqualify you and that is you and God. Other than that, no one can take away what you have been given. The gifts and calls of God are without repentance which means you always have a shot if there is breath in your lungs. Isn't that wonderful? That is enough to make you shout Glory Hallelujah! It is true Jesus has prepared you for such a time as this.

Now, let's examine some characters in the bible that were anointed. The first person who was anointed above all others is Jesus Christ of Nazareth, the Messiah. He is the anointed one, our savior and Lord of all who has all power in

His hands. He has all authority and the one who poured His spirit out upon the whole world so that we can be anointed and appointed. Jesus had the anointed to save the world. Anointings are assignments. Jesus was anointed Messiah. Jesus was anointed savior. Believe it or not each one of you reading this book is anointed with an assignment. Right now, declare out loud the following, "I am anointed with a heavenly assignment". You have an assignment. In 1 Corinthians 12:4-6 it says, "Now, there are varieties of gifts, but the same Spirit, and there are varieties of service, but the same Lord; and there are varieties of activities, but it is the same God who empowers them all in everyone". Now, I'm going to add something that is going to help many of you, there are varieties of ministries. I just set so many people free right now. Now, you are not going to compare yourself to another ministry any longer. You are not going to copy of anyone else any longer; however, you are going to have similarities with other ministries. Some of you will be apostles, prophets, evangelists, pastors, and teachers. Some of you will be able to do different things. Just know this there are differences or variety of ministries, but the same Lord. There are diversities of activities, but the same God who works all in all. Therefore, God has something specific for you to do. You have an assignment. Now listen, anointings can be for a small town, a pastor of one church, or a pastor of multiple churches. You could be an apostle where you are planting churches in various locations. You can be a regional apostolic authority. You can be a prophet to a whole nation. You can be a prophet to a city or town.

You see what I'm saying? You might an anointed business owner or apostolic business owner. You must understand, God has given you an assignment. You have something that you were assigned to do, but that makes you no more or no less than anyone else.

A problem we have in the body of Christ, one that I too was guilty of, is we look at other men and women of God with envy. I mean we start wanting to be them. I understand having a spiritual father/mother, or mentor, people who inspire us. I am not saying that is wrong. You follow them as they follow Christ. Now, catch this, most likely, you are attracted to what you are. For example, I used to chase down deliverance ministers because I loved the tenacity. I love the warfare aspect. I love that stuff. I later found out that I have a lot of same similarities and giftings. I was not exactly like them, but they carried something that I liked that I had on the inside of me. If you have been following The Supernatural Life long enough, many of you will know that I love to evangelize, cast out demons, and to prophesy. Some people say I am a prophetic evangelist, evangelistic prophet, or an apostle. I am whatever God needs me to be. All I know is that I am doing what God has called me to do. I know one of the ways I was able to see the anointed on my life was I looked to people who had a similar anointing. Not necessarily people with the same anointing because I was assigned to different things. I understood that they have their assignment while I have mine, yet the anointing was similar. It does not mean it is your anointing. Look at Saul and David. Both were kings but were totally different. Look at Elijah and Elisha. Both were prophets who had similar gifts, but with very different characteristics.

Now, let's examine King David. Oftentimes, the one who is truly anointed, is not going to be the one who you think it is. If you walk into a room of people, you will notice the tall, dark, and handsome guy and fail to notice the little, pale, and crazy looking guy. For some reason, God chooses the one who looks pale and crazy looking. Look at John the Baptist. He had locust in his beard, yet he was anointed, and referred to as being greater than all the other prophets. Why? He was prophesying the coming of Jesus Christ. Oftentimes, it is the person who we overlook. The last one we would consider. The one who is down and out who no one thinks God will raise up. God is known to use the foolish things to confound the wise. You do not want to be quick to point your finger at someone with laughter because in a moment, God can raise them up. You can never know the heart of man, only Jesus knows. He does not look at the outward appearance but upon the heart. David was anointed because of his heart. The bible says that he was a man after God's heart. Your heart will determine the anointing, and the appointment. A good heart gets good things, but a bad heart will cause you to be like Saul.

In 1 Samuel 16:7-13, it says, "But the Lord said to Samuel, "Do not look on his appearance or on the height of his stature, because I have rejected him. For the Lord sees not as man sees; man looks on the outward appearance, but the Lord looks on the heart. Then Jesse called Abinadab and made him pass before Samuel. And he said, neither has the Lord chosen this one. And Jesse made Shammah pass by. And he said, neither has the Lord chosen this one. And Jesse made seven of his sons pass before Samuel. And Samuel said to Jesse, the Lord has not chosen these. Then Samuel said to Jesse, are all your sons here? And he said, there remains yet the youngest, but behold he is keeping the sheep. And Samuel said to Jesse, send and get him, for we will not sit down till he comes here. And he sent and brought him in. Now he was ruddy and had beautiful eyes and was handsome. And the Lord said, arise anoint him, for this is he. Then Samuel took the horn of oil and anointed him in the midst of his brothers. And the spirit of the Lord rushed upon David from that day forward. And Samuel rose up and went to Ramah".

What is cool about this passage is that King David was in the sheep fold, hanging out, fighting lions and bares. After he was anointed, he went back to fighting lions and bears. He did not go straight into his call. Listen, just because you have been anointed, does not mean you are going to be automatically appointed. David was anointed, but he wasn't appointed right away. There was someone else still in that appointed position. He could not take that role that he anointed for until that appointed one, Saul, was taken down. David recognized that Saul was the appointed one and waited until he came off the throne. When David was able to take the throne, he officially walked into the appointed time of his anointing. There is an appointed time of your anointing. I'll repeat that again, there is an appointed time of your anointing. You can try to override it or do it in your own strength, but it will manifest when it is ready. There are times of preparation that must occur. David had to go through preparation. He went through tough trials and tribulations. He not only had to fight lions and bears but stand in front of the deadly giant. David had to conquer the giant. He had to go through assassination attempts from Saul. Had to go through things that crushed things that needed to be crushed and broken out of his life so that he can become the humble man God intended. Thus, when he was humble, there is no way pride could have entered his heart. Of course, he made mistakes, but he always came back to what mattered which was his heart towards God. Even in moments of failure, Saul refused to repent and humble himself. He refused to acknowledge his mistakes and flaws because he took a position, which led him to being rejected by God.

Now, David had an assignment to show Israel that there is a good king. He was definitely not Jesus. Jesus is the perfect King. On the hand, David did not do the best all the time of being a good example. What he did have was a heart after God so much so that Jesus was born through his lineage. Just think about that for a moment. That's just amazing. Even in the midst of his flaws, sins, and tribulations, he never lost the anointing because of his heart. Listen, you don't lose the anointing. You lose the anointing because you pride. You lose the anointing because you refuse to turn from wickedness. David always had his heart towards God. David's heart was never far from God. David said Lord forgive me, search my heart, show my anxieties for I have sinned against you. When you can acknowledge your sin and problems before God, the anointing will never leave. The anointing will only increase and grow through trials and tribulations. It will not leave. You will not be Ichabod; you know the spirit will not depart and leave you forever. You always got a chance to repent. So, if someone comes up to you says, you are not anointed anymore, this is not the old covenant anymore. This is the new covenant which means you will always have a change to turn back. Now, if you have been given over to a reprobate mind and you are in trouble. If you transgress to the point of no return, my question would be, "Did you really know Jesus"? I know personally, I have been through some tough moments in my life, I would find myself running right back to the altar of Christ. I can't stay away from the Lord because He is so good. David was anointed king to lead Israel and went through a lot of hard times. Don't think because you are anointed, you are not going to have battles. Please don't get it twisted, because the power of God is moving through your life, that you are the almighty power ranger for Jesus. Yes, you are powerful in Christ, but it is for His glory. You want the appointing right? You want to be used by Jesus, correct? Then, you just signed up to go do through some stuff. You just got signed up to go through some breaking and molding moments in your life. The anointing is a beautiful thing, but it is intended to also stir everything that isn't supposed to be in you up. I mean it will stir and cause to manifest everything that is not supposed to be inside of you. It comes up to me which is why you see young preachers and young people get puffed up with pride and fall. The Bible says not to place your hands hastily on a novice unless they become puffed up with pride and fall. Why is that? God knows when they are in an anointed position, that the anointing is going to stir everything up on the inside of them up. Why would you make them a public spectacle or appoint them too hastily? Being quick to promote or appoint them is going to blow him up or destroy them. That is why the Bible says don't be hasty in giving positions to them. Let people process and develop. Now, there was a moment in my life where I did not process appropriately which caused a lot of unnecessary trials and tribulations. Thank God I took the King David position, and said Lord, forgive me, I give up and don't want to do things my way any longer. Please never be hasty to jump into a platform. Let God work through you. Go back to fighting the lions and bears. Go back to finding Goliath and stoning him. Desire to learn, process, and grow. If you are a young person watching this right now, it doesn't mean that you are not going to be a preacher. If you are a teenager, this does not mean that you are not going to be a preacher. This does not mean that you cannot go into the streets and evangelize. Of course, everybody watching this can be a preacher in the streets. You absolutely can, but do not go standing in front of men and women of God preaching a lot of things and your life is still compromised. Now you are exalted in front of men and women with influence. I have a big stage right now. I have to live a very consecrated, Jesus loving life. I have battles. I have things I cannot compromise anymore. There is no more compromise for me. God has exalted me in the season. I must uphold this platform for His glory. There is no one else to give glory to but Jesus Christ. So, remember these things when you are appointed because you have a job. When God exalts you, your job is to make sure Jesus is glorified in everything you do.

William Branham, who was a great man of God, many people know his story about angels who came to speak to him. He had some of the most extraordinary words of knowledge and movements overall happen through him. But there was a moment in his life where he believed that he was the Elijah to come. What happened? The power and the platform went to the guy's head. Even to this day you have what's called Branhamites, people who still believe he is Elijah. Of course, that is not true. As a result, his platform was taken from him because he tried to go into the wrong assignment. Look at John Alexander Dowie which had Zion City which great healings broke out in their meetings. He even fell off the map. When you take on the wrong role, you fall and will essentially mess up. People, stay in your lane. When you know you are anointed for something, and it is working, stay in your lane. Do what you are supposed to do. Do not try to enter an area you are not called to because that is pride trying to come into your heart. Pride will make you want to become something you are not called to be. Do what you are called to do. Be happy. If you are a Christian baker, be that, especially if the Lord is blessing your business abundantly. Stay in your assignment. Stay in your assignment because this is bigger than us. Stay in your assignment and you will always be in Godly alignment.

I will show you a man of God who was anointed for a specific purpose, and he had the characteristics. God is looking for people who carry certain characteristics for certain assignments. I am an ex-cage fighter and ex-correctional officer. Well, if there is a war going down, a demon that does not want to let go, probably God is going send ole Danny Boy here to cut its head off. God will probably send a sweet little ole thing in there to do the work unless she has got some fire in there you do not see. You never know; however, God is looking for people with certain characteristics and demeanors to do specific things because we are the body of Christ. Always tell people I need you. I tell people all the time I need you as much as you need me. I can't do this by myself. We are the body of Christ. I know that I don't have what you have, and I am ok with that. I don't want to have what you have when I have enough. I want to learn from what you have and deposit some of what you have into my life. Jesus Christ is the one true everything.

In 2 Kings 9:1-13, it says "Then Elisha the prophet called one of the songs of the prophets and said to him, 'Tie up your garments, and take this flask of oil in your hand, and go to Ramoth-gilead. And when you arrive, look there for Jesu the son of Jehoshaphat, son of Nimshi. And go in and have him rise from among his fellows and lead him to an inner chamber. Then take the flask of oil and pour it on his head and say, 'Thus says the Lord, I anoint you king

70

over Israel.' Then open the door and flee; do not longer.' So, the young man, the servant of the prophet, went to Ramoth-gilead. And when he came, behold the commanders of the army were in council. And he said, 'I have a word for you, O commander.' And Jesus said, 'To which of us all?' And he said, 'To you, O commander.' So, he arose and went into the house. And the young man of the Lord, over Israel. And you shall strike down the house of Ahab your master, so that I may avenge on Jezebel the blood of my servants the prophets, and the blood of all the servants of the Lord. For the whole house of Ahab shall perish, and I will cut off from Ahab every male, bond or free, in Israel. And I will make the house of Ahab like the house of Jeroboam the son of Nebat, and like the house of Baasha the son of Ahijah. And the dogs shall eat Jezebel in the territory of Jezreel, and none shall bury her.' Then he opened the door and fled. When Jehu came out to the servants of his master, they said to him, 'Is all well? Why did this mad fellow come to you?' And he said to them, 'You know the fellow and his talk.' And they said, 'That is not true; tell us now.' And he said, 'Thus and so he spoke to me, saying, 'Thus says the Lord, I anoint you king over Israel.' Then in haste every man of them took his garment and put it under him on the bare steps, and they blew the trumpet and proclaimed, 'Jehu is king'."

Jehu was chosen to take out Jezebel. Now, let's examine Jehu's characteristics for a moment. It is said that Jehu drove his chariot like a madman. He was wild. The prophet who had to anointed him probably took a double look at his surroundings as well as Jehu. I would be thinking let me anoint this guy real quick and get up out of here. The question is why did God choose a man like Jehu? Why didn't God just have Elijah take out Jezebel. Elijah had a seed of fear and got scared of Jezebel. He did not have the privilege of wiping out Jezebel but instead he took out her prophets of Baal. So, God brought forth the conquering behind Elijah which is Jehu. Now Jehu had the characteristics that was needed to take the witch, Jezebel out. God knew that Jehu would stand firm in front of her in boldness. God knew that he wouldn't be moved by her seduction. God used Jehu's characteristics to defeat her. Sometimes we as Christians get offended at the people that God uses. Guess what? God does not care what you think, instead He cares about what His assignment is for that person; therefore, we need to get over what we think about other men and women of God. Let them fulfill their assignment instead of judging the man or woman of God. Why don't we stand firm and get into our assignment? Do not judge a man who is already in their assignment. Do not judge a woman who is already in their assignment. If that person is just doing their job and you don't understand why God is using them in that way, He may be using that circumstance to get you out of your head. We must stop trying to control and figure everything out.

Jehu was chosen, yet he was not what people thought God would use to take out Jezebel. To God, he fit the characteristics and overall, what was needed for that time. If you notice in scripture, even after that time, Jehu went and took everything out. I mean he wrecked house. If he was alive today, he would have offended everybody. I mean, Chris-

72

tians today are so entitled and incredibly soft. If Jehu swept through, they would be crying on the ground complaining about what he said to them. Jehu was a king. His assignment came with authority to go do what he had to do. He was focused on his assignment. You see, when a prophet comes and gives you the word of the Lord regarding your assignment, he is going to give you the details of what you are supposed to do. A prophet told Jehu that he was anointed to carry out a specific assignment. If you are a man or woman of God that is about your father's business, thank you Jesus. God has given you your assignment; therefore, you are determined to stick to it and stay the course.

Another example in the bible of a man who understood his assignment is Paul. He said my name is Paul an apostle to the Gentiles. He knew his assignment. He did not gloat over anyone. Sometimes we have issues with people because they know who they are in Christ, and what they are assigned to do. God going to choose people at times that you will not agree with. Sometimes God will let things happen that will blow your mind because he's working intricacies. God is a wonder worker and way maker. God has to choose certain things, move certain ways in order to get the assignment done. I can reflect to a time when I sat under a great revivalist for 3 years. That man was hard on me, but I was also a prideful and rebellious kid that did not listen to his mommy or daddy. I was really jacked up. It took a very strong hearted man of God to beat me into the submission of the Lord. You know what I mean? It took hard times for me to get the fear of the Lord in my life. I thank God for that man because if I was not put in front of him, I would not be where I am today. It takes certain men and women of God in your life to break things off you.

People are also assigned to your anointing. When you have anointed and appointed, God will assign people to you. Certain people are assigned to you for you to remove things from them. Some of you reading this may be wondering, what if that person is manipulative? Here's the thing, if you are in front of a servant of God that is controlling and manipulating; although, that does not make it right, God is trying to expose something in your heart that needs to be removed. God uses all things. It is in the bible. He uses all things for the good of those who love Him. If you are looking for man, like a Saul, you are going to find one. If you have daddy issues, you are going to end up in from of a Saul and the Saul is going to bring you to the real father. Did you catch that? Remember, we are here to know our assignment. I believe this right now, that anyone reading this book that does not know their assignment will begin to know it. I believe the Holy Spirit is going to speak to some of you and provide clarity on what you need to do. He is going to touch, change, and speak to many of you.

What are you good at? Why are you on this earth? Here are some questions you can ask yourself to find out what you are anointed and appointed to do. What am I here to do? What am I good at? Some people might be saying thinking I do not know. Well, you are going to keep not knowing be-cause a double minded person is unstable in all their ways.

How can they expect this receive anything from God? You might be saying that you need a man or woman of God to come prophesy to you. No, you need to crack open your bible and get the prophetic word from the pages. Doing such will allow you to hear the word of God for your life. You cannot watch YouTube videos all day to figure out your assignment. You might get attracted to things that are like your assignment, but it is the word of God that will reveal it. Today is the day of assignment. Today is the day of appointing and anointing. Today is the day of Grace. Today is the day of your appointed time. Today is the day of no rush. Today is the day of saying Lord, I will have patience and joy. I will have long suffering because I know that you are working things out of my heart. I know you are working things out of my life.

HOW TO KNOW IF YOU HAVE A DEMON

As I travel all over the world conducting revivals, we seeing many demons coming out of Christians. Sometimes other ministers ask why do we talk so much about demons? Well, one of the things Satan wants you to do is believe that he does not exist because then he can get into your ear. If you know about the enemy, his tactics, you will know how to remove him from your life. It is good to know your enemy and make people aware of his schemes. We love the spirit realm when it is dealing with Jesus, heaven, and such, but there is a war raging in the spirit that we cannot afford to overlook either. Now, we know the war has been won, yet according to scripture, the enemy still roams like a roaring lion seeking whom he may devour. Satan is a psychopath, driven by insanity. His goal is to try to make as many people crazy as he is and unfortunately, many fall to his schemes. So, there is another side to the realm of the spirit where Satan and his angels reside. Some people call it the second heaven. Now, there is the first heaven, which represents earth, the second, which is the demonic realm, and the third, which is where God resides. Thus, we who are alive reside in the first heaven and battle with the spirits that reside in the second. Now, there are certain issues we should have as Christians. Let's just be real, we as Christians, should not have demons. Can a Christian have a demon? The answer is of course. Christians can many demons if they desire. They can eat them like candy if they want to, but should they have them? No. The question is why do they have a demon? I believe, we as the church, have not brought the full revelation of the finished gospel into the forefront. We have not brought the full power of the gospel to the forefront either; therefore, as a result, we have Christians that continue to suffer. Now, some Christians just choose to make ignorant mistakes which is on them, not the church. However, if we would teach better and let it be known that there is an enemy that wants to destroy us, then I believe we would do better. We need revelatory teaching on this topic. We need to tell people how they can get demons, how to stay away from them, and why you shouldn't commit sin. We need to know what the weight of sin feels like and what is Godly sorrow and the fear of the Lord. We need to know what holiness, righteous, and purity mean. It is easy to say that Jesus has made us holy pure and righteous, but it is another thing to understand it. Again, you can say it, but you must become it. How do you become those things? You spend time with the one who gave it to you. When you spend with the one who gave it to you, no longer will you need to worry about it all day because you just understand it. You are holy as He is holy. Righteous as He is righteous. You are pure as He is pure. It is just that simple. When you understand Jesus and who He is, his Glory and the presence that He brings, it keeps you in a place where you do not want to be in sin. On the other hand, if you do have sin in your life, you're convicted to the core, and you want to put it away. You want to change.

We have a defeated enemy of our soul. That enemy still has power through lies, fear, and the only way he has access to you is through a legal binding contract. He must have a way in your life. You would have to give him a way in. Some of us are ignorant because our family has exposed us to things that taught us how to give the enemy legal access. As a result of the negative exposure, we now have to renew our minds in Christ according to Romans 12:2. Also, in 2 Corinthians 5:17, it says that "There if anyone is in Christ, he is a new creation; old things have passed away; behold, all things have become new". You no longer have to live as a dead man any longer. The dead man is dead and the new man has arisen through Christ Jesus. Unfortunately, the truth is that we like to resurrect that dead man and that is where the enemy likes to play. Being lukewarm is also another area where the enemy loves to play. You cannot play with God and play with Satan; it does not work. He is in the middle, in fact, he loves to abide in the middle. Jesus said I rather you be hot or cold. What is He saying? He is saying do not play games. Jesus said let your yes be yes and your no be no which is the same concept. Do not be in the middle. The middle is not a good place to be. Look the second heaven is in the middle. Again, the middle ground is Satan's playground. A person who is cold has already sold out to the other side; therefore, the devil does not have to worry about them. Those individuals are already serving him, so he does not have to bother them. A person who is lukewarm is his perfect playground and this where the enemy can make their life a living hell because these individuals are professing God with their mouth, but their actions are reflecting something completely different. Please allow this teaching to convict your heart causing you to return to God. Allow it to push you into on fire Christian for the glory of God. It's time for us to burn for Jesus. We need revival because the world is getting crazier and crazier. We need to wake up and get on fire for Jesus Christ. We possess the answer to society's issues.

In Luke 8:1-3, it says "Soon afterward he went on through cities and villages, proclaiming and bringing the good news of the kingdom of God. And the twelve were with him, and also some women who had been healed of evil spirits and infirmities; Mary, called Magdalene, from whom seven demons had gone out, and Joanna, the wife of Chuza, Herod's household manager, and Susanna, and many others, who provided for them out of their means". What I love about this passage is the ones that Jesus healed and delivered were the same ones who funded his kingdom work. The pharisees would have a problem with that accusing him of taking money from heathens. Now, Mary Magdalene had 7 demons and all with a specific assignment. The bible does not reveal what spirits were inside of her, but each had distinct qualities that was causing her to behavior a particular way. Jesus later comes on the scene and completely delivers her from those spirits. As a result, she chooses to follow Him and do the same things He is doing. Jesus gives her authority and power to cast out demons as well.

Obviously, more than one demon can be inside of a person. People can have multiple demons. We see that in ministry all the time. Jesus cast seven demons out of her. How did Jesus do it? I think about it at times because we have ministers that operate in deliverance, and they say all you have to do is say "Come Out" and the demons will leave. I agree that can happen but let's just be real, there were seven demons inside of her. Jesus knew there were seven demons there and He cast seven demons out. So, there was probably a process of deliverance with Mary Magdalene. I don't know that 100%. Don't hold me to it, but what I do know is that you cannot apply a method to how things are done in the area of deliverance. It is very important to be led by the Holy Spirit. Sometimes we will look at another person and says that person is not delivering right or that person does not know how many demons a person has. Sometimes you will not know what demons are inside of them or how bad they are suffering. Sometimes it takes a short time, an hour, or multiple hours to help someone get free. I believe that we can get faith to a level that you can get people completely free on the first attempt. The key is faith to achieve that kind of result. Again, I'm not saying that deliverance must be short or long because every case is different. If the person is getting free, we should not get hung up on method. Jesus said that we have been given measures of faith.

In Luke 8:26-39, in this passage there was a man that had legions of demons. After being set free he becomes an instant evangelist. This man had all kind of things going on and what I love about Jesus is that He hits him with the one

81

hit KO shot which causes every demon to leave. I mean it all came out of this man's life through one encounter with Jesus. Again, every situation is different. I've noticed in my life; every situation is different. I do not put a period on a method. Some people say never negotiate with demons but in this passage of scripture Jesus negotiated. Jesus was going to send them back to the pit but they pleaded with Him to send them into the pigs and He did. Although, there was a moment of exchange, the devil still lost again because the pigs went over the cliff. I love it because Jesus has always showed the enemy up. He showed him on the cross, when he was in the wilderness being tempted, and he showed him up with the pigs to name a few. Jesus is going to show Him in a major way when he returns and raptures the saints.

We see in this passage that people can be oppressed by demons. A pastor that I was with recently had people asking him if Christians can have a demon? Can Christians who are endowed with the Holy Ghost have demons in them as well? My answer is that they should not but they do. How is that possible you might be asking? Well, there are Christians that are filled with the Holy Spirit that have sickness and disease inside of them. I mean Christians even have sickness. Should they be sick? No. Should they have diseases? No, but they do, and we must pray for them and get him healed. In scripture, there was a boy that was sick, and people asked why is this boy in this condition? Jesus replied that it was not because of his parents but for the glory of God. Thus, we see people in the Bible that have demonization problems. So, I want to say that I believe in salvation. I believe in water baptism and the repentance of sins. I believe in the baptism of the Holy Spirit. I believe in the gifts of the Holy Spirit. I believe that we should all be operating in the power of the Holy spirit. I also believe we should know the word of God. I believe we should be in relationship with Jesus Christ and walk a life that gives Him glory.

Now, I'm going to give you ten signs that will help those of you reading this book identify if you are dealing with a demon. Number one, you are seeing the same cycles that followed your family bloodline, following you. You are participating in the same sins that they were committing. We call those generational curses. We also call those familiar spirits which are spirits that follow the family bloodline. If you notice that you carry the same sickness or disease that your family has carried. If you notice that you fell into the same sins that your mommy or daddy fell into, and you are unable to stop. It is a good chance you are dealing with a demon. You must have humility to get free from demons. You will not get free unless you have humility. You will not get unless you are transparent. Just the other day a pastor asked me to tell my testimony. I told him and that I was going to tell it as real and raw as I possibly can. People were quite surprised that I was so raw with my testimony. My response to them is that I must expose myself so that no one can expose me later. People love to attempt to use my past against me, but I am like you can't because I have already used it. I use it as my testimony; therefore, you can't touch my past because I already gave it to Jesus.

You must real and not care about what people think. Who cares what people know? The devil lives in the secrets of man. You must let the secrets go because there are none in the Kingdom. Now, if you have a matter that is between you and your spouse, that's the holy place that should not be shared with everyone. Don't be scared to release your testimony, yet be wise as serpents, and harmless as a dove. Number 2, you have no self-control over your emotions or physical actions. You try as hard as possible not to participate in sin. You try as hard as possible not to get emotionally unstable, rejected, angry, and quick reacting. Someone says something to you that you do not like, and you are quick to come back on them really fast. These are big signs that you have no self-control and that means that you are probably demonized. Let's just be real. Let's just call it is what it is. Because you can't control yourself, there's no self-control. Self-control is a fruit of the spirit; therefore, if you know that you have no self-control, your emotions get the best of you, and you get super angry, it is a demon. You may feel yourself getting depressed and can't control it. You try to pull yourself out of your emotions, but you find yourself physically doing stuff that you should not be doing. Even though you want to stop, you really can't. Another example is involving people who are addicted to drugs. Many will say I want to stop but unable to quit. All of these are signs that you are probably demonized. It is important to note that you cannot beat a demon in your own strength. You need Jesus Christ to come in and do His job. You need Him to send a deliverer.

Number 3, you have intrusive thoughts and immoral dreams. Intrusive thoughts are ones that get access to you and talk to you, but they should not have access. Thoughts that should be able to talk to you, but you hear them all the time. An example is an intrusive thought that you hate yourself. You hear someone tell you that they do not like you and now you just keep hearing it over and over. Immoral dreams are sexual dreams, having visitations in your dreams, doing things you shouldn't be doing. These are great signs that you could have some demonization going on and they have access through things like pornography and immoral affairs. If you give the enemy access, he will be able to intrude and do awful things in your life. Because the demons is inside, it can cause you to do things that makes you become condemned and full of shame. Now, just because you experience moments of sin, that does not mean that you are demonized automatically. I am talking about more significant or chronic cases that prevents people from being able to crucify the flesh. Your flesh will not get crucified. You fasted 40 days and still nothing has changed. You have done everything you can, and it is just still there. Well, that is when casting out that spirit must happen. The words up and out need to be spoke over you. You just need simple deliverance. Just get deliverance. Some of you have been fasting in works, thinking that thinking that your works is going to get you free. That is not how things work. It is the grace of God that sets you free. He freely sets us free because he loves us.

85

Number 4, here's a good one, there is paranormal activity happening in your house. This can mean there is a demonic attachment that came through occult activity from your past. People who confessed to practicing Ouija boards, using new age crystals, and other occultic activities admit to seeing stuff move in their house. Sometimes it is cases of things disappearing, such as car keys you cannot find or feeling something attack you. Well, that just means you probably opened something up in the occult. You could also have a generational spirit attached to you that you need to get free from. So, paranormal activity, poltergeists are demons that try to put fear into you and aim to destroy your life.

Number 5, you never prosper no matter what you do in the natural. You give, give, and give, oftentimes for many years but never see yourself break out of poverty. You feel stuck and often wonder why you cannot seem to break free. This type of scenario occurs when a demon has a legal right to block your blessing. And you must figure out where it is derived from, what is the root cause? Where is that giving that spirit a legal right to your life? Your thought life could be the root cause because the bible says as a man thinks in his heart so is he. You could be thinking a certain way that could be give a legal right for the enemy to keep you poor. There could be just a spiritual attachment that occurred subliminally meaning you don't even know is there. I was. I can use me as it as a testimony. I can remember days where although I was not poor, I always remained in a state of just having enough. We should not settle with just having enough. We should have more than enough so that you can help the Kingdom. Frugal giving, being scared to give, or just the wrong perception of giving are all signs that you could be demonized. I have noticed in my life that the more I give, God loves to give back to me the more. Did you know that Jesus had a treasurer that accompanied him, who name was Judas? Jesus had people giving him riches. Look at Mary Magdalene; again, a woman who supported his ministry and gave to the people in the towns they visited. Even in the midst of Jesus receiving, he was always giving. In fact, He gave everything.

I have a testimony of poverty. I had so many bills because I grew up in perversion and pride. I was a young Christian full of pride and ego which was keeping me poor. It was causing me trouble. Until we humble ourselves and realize that poverty is not our portion, we will not be able to break away from it. I want to be a blessing to others. We all should want to be that way; therefore, we should be in a place that's open to receive the blessings of God. I'm personally tired of poor minded Christianity. I see too many poor minded Christians that never receive breakthrough which is why the Bible says the poor will always be among us. I declare to you right now that you do not have to be demonized resulting in things being stole from you. Do not be settled with being in lack. Do not allow a religious spirit to speak to you and cause you to believe that it is ok to be poor.

Number 6, there is always a path of sabotage everywhere you go even though your intentions are completely opposite. So, you walk around in life and notice sabotage follows you. Your credit card does not work right when you need it, things start breaking around you, messes up the things start breaking around are examples of sabotage. Odd stuff just keeps happening all around you and you can't seem to understand it. Why is this breaking? Why am I always having things mess up around me? That means you could have a spirit of sabotage lurking. I've noticed people that get involved in pornography, perversion, and immorality have a spirit of sabotage. I It also brings a spirit of poverty into their life. I have also noticed that everything around them begins to fall apart. They even self-sabotage even though that isn't the intent of their heart. Sometimes this spirit can travel through the generational bloodline. Sometimes sabotage is all around them that they become prideful, refusing to admit what is happening in their life. Until they humble themselves, the sabotage is going to be in their life just like any other sin.

I used to self-sabotage as well because of the way I grew up. In fact, my life was sabotaged from the very beginning. I come from a broken family, and I just started sabotaging everything around me. Anything I touched resulted in destruction. I just had destruction all around me, because of how I grew up and what I was exposed to from my youth. Anger is another thing that brings sabotage in along with rebellion. Rebellion is as the sin of witchcraft. Overall, if you have sabotage in your life, these can open doors to demonization.

Number 7 is another way to know if you have demon. This is one that I run into with Christians all the time. I was in the gym recently and Christian lady told me that she had bad knees. You should not have bad knees. Nonetheless, if you are always sick, you might have a demon. A spirit of infirmity is always in your life. You recover from one sickness and then the next moment, you get another. Every time you look up, you are always sick, always getting the flu. This is a good indication you may be demonized in that area of infirmity. I believe many of you reading this book right now are dealing with the spirit of infirmity. You can relate to always being sick. You always have something wrong with you. This means that somewhere in your life, perhaps in your bloodline, you are carrying the same sickness and infirmity that has been in your family. Sickness is a lie from the devil. Your portion is not sickness, like your portions not poverty. Your portion is health and faith. We live by faith. If you are sick today, take the faith to be healed. Jesus healed and delivered all people.

Number 8, you never have energy or joy in your life. Have you ever said, "I'm just so tired"? Yet, you are not doing enough to be so tired and not have energy. There is no energy or joy in your life, and you are just living. You are just making it through each day. You are never happy about things. There is no excitement. These are good signs that are dealing with a demon that is holding you down and placing a heavy burden on your life.

Number 9, you never have relationships that thrive. Your relationship life sucks. Let's just say it like it is. I know some people don't like to suck word, but it is what it is. It sucks is another word for 'not good'. So, your relationships are bad. There is always mess and none of your relationships thrive. I am one that understands persecution, trials, and tribulations. I'm not talking about that aspect. I am also not talking about the relationships that end because of poor decisions people make. I am referring to people who never seem to have relationships that thrive. I'm talking about the relationships that you are causing issues in, yet you are not trying to. You ever notice sometimes you'll be around people and suddenly, they just get mad at you for no reason? Well, that is a demon pushing people away from you. I have been in relationships with people that I would notice something on them that is pushing me away. It is like you want to be close to that individual, but you can't get close. You will even tell that person that you are going to call them back, but you never do. It is typically a spirit on them that is trying to make that person feel isolated and rejected.

Number 10, you can't leave a toxic relationship. This is a good one for everybody. You feel attached to toxic relationships. You want to let that relationship go, but you just can't. It is like your mind is telling you yes, but your body is telling you no. Your mind is saying go and never return, but your body is saying stay. This is how you know you are in a toxic relationship, and something is wrong. This does not just apply to dating or marriage, but this can apply to friendships, or simply a person that is manipulating you. There could be a person in your life saying 'I need you today. I need your prayers'. Every day that person needs you because their life is messed up. That is a toxic relationship man. There is no thriving there and it is complete unhealthy. All they do is take, take, take from you and everything around them is destruction. For some reason, you just feel like you must be their savior. That is a toxic relationship that you need to get out of your life. If you are married, I am not saying leave your spouse. You can't leave. I know how people think so I am going to be very clear. You can't just leave your spouse instead you will need to pray and win the battle. Please learn from me because I made those mistakes. You don't want to make the same mistakes because it is a very painful place to be in. If you are attracted to toxic relationships, you she just might have a demon.

All 9 of these examples represent signs that a person is dealing with a demon. There are many other examples in addition to these mentioned. I hope you have been encouraged and learned from how to get the enemy out of your life. I truly want to see people free. After years of toiling, going through various trials and tribulations, figuring some things out the hard way, I truly desire to make the road easier for others to travel. I want to make sure that you don't travel that broad road that leads to destruction but instead stay on that narrow path that leads to life. I want to see everybody thrive. Remember, God resists the proud and exalts the humble. So, resists the proud mindset and humble yourself and watch God set you free from every demonic influence in your life.

HOW TO DO
SELF-DELIVERANCE

I believe self-deliverance is very easy to do but it requires some humility. I believe after you have read this chapter, you are going to receive the freedom you have been seeking. Oftentimes, we run all over the place looking for deliverance and freedom. Nothing is wrong with that because you are determined to receive freedom wherever you can get it. Humility will lead you to get freedom because you are willing to deny yourself to get what God has for you. Obviously true freedom can only come through Jesus Christ because He is the only true deliverer. Any other way is going to lead you down a bad path of destruction.

I have quoted this scripture before, but in James 4:6 it says that "God resists the proud but gives grace to the humble". If you are humble, you are going to get what you need of the Lord. Humility is key. When it comes to self-deliverance, you cannot approach it with a proud horn. If you have pride, the only way you are truly going to get deliverance is to be exposed. In proverbs 21:2 says, "Every way of a man is right in his own eyes, but the Lord weights the heart". God truly knows your heart. If you are trying to walk in your prayer closet, get self-deliverance with pride in your heart only to go out and proclaim to the world that you did it all by yourself, then guess what? You are probably not going to get the deliverance you were looking for yourself. God will probably lead you to a place where you are going to be exposed for his glory. Not exposed to bring shame, guilt, and condemnation upon you. Exposure is not a bad thing. Personally, I love talking about every experience that I've had with Jesus Christ including self-deliverance as well as being delivered from others. I mean you guys know that even my own wife has delivered me. I've been delivered in front of a whole crowd of people before. I just don't care. However, it comes, let it come.

Self-deliverance is a revelatory thing because it comes from being in relationship with Jesus Christ, dwelling in His word and prayer. As you do these things, what's going to happen is revelation will come upon you, and you will receive wisdom that only comes from the Lord. Wisdom that comes from the father of lights. You are going to receive divine revelation that is going to bring you deliverance. For example, I was walking around one day, and I was thinking about the generations on my father's side and how they just keep failing at things. So, I said I'm sick of this and the Lord gave me a revelation of why this kept happening. I didn't realize there was a demonic stronghold in my life that came through my bloodline. I just knew I was tired of it. I just said, "I'm sick of this. Hey Lord, I need deliverance from this. I don't care how you do it, but I need it to happen now'. You see have done self-delivered in the in the past and understood that He who is in me is greater than He who is in the world, which means that His spirit dwells within me. Therefore, if anything else is inside of me other than His spirit, He will push it on out. Only one master can truly own a house because the other master will kick the other one out. It takes grace to receive self-deliverance. You must ask for God's grace because you need to receive this freedom that He promised you at the cross of Calvary. When I received this revelation and began to command every demonic thing that is attached to it to leave me now, suddenly, I felt it come up. I just released that thing and it started screaming out. It came out in tears, snot, and vomit. I was completely set free. Now listen, I saw the results of my self-deliverance. Sometimes people like to do take the glory and boast about their self-deliverance. Also, you do not see the results of their self-deliverance. Whenever anybody goes through any type of deliverance there is always breakthrough on the other side. You will see the victory. You will see the testimony of their deliverance.

So, self-deliverance requires humility. Self-deliverance requires revelation that comes through the father in heaven, which is brought by the word. It is brought through the truth that is found in Jesus Chris. It can also come through other men and women of God. You know, even reading this book, God can release divine revelation that can release deliverance in your life. Once you receive the revelation, determine that is time to be free. Repent and renounce whatever it is that has been afflicting you. When you are doing self-deliverance, you must first, repent which requires you turning away from every lie you came into agreement with over your life. When you turn from that sin, the Lord will see your heart and you will feel the grace of God come upon your life. You will then be released from that demonic spirit. Now, the next part will take faith in action. You will say with authority, "I command right now this demonic thing that is hindering my life, whatever its name is, whatever it is attached to, I command you in the name of Jesus Christ of Nazareth to come up and out of me now". When you say these words with the grace of God upon you, it will start to release off you. You may fill a burden or weight leave. You will either breathe out or yawn. Some will cough or snot. Others may cry. There are many ways you can experience freedom. I mean anywhere there's an opening it can come out, but you will receive what you asked for and you will experience that entity leaving your life. Afterwards you will see the result of your self-deliverance. I wouldn't release the testimony until you see the results. I see the results of my self-deliverances. You can just look at the fruit. Remember, a good tree bears good fruit. You will see the good fruit. Guess what's going to happen? You are going to testify about it and people are going to see it too.

What I am sharing with is from personal revelation of self-deliverance. Again, I've done it and it not only worked, but I have seen the results in my life. Amen. This is for the glory of Jesus Christ. Although I was able to self-delivery, there was other areas of my life that required men and women of God, or my own wife, or whoever was a believer near me, praying for me to be set free. If self-deliverance is all you are going to do because you do not want anyone touching you, then you are full of pride and will not receive deliverance. You need to go ahead and just find somebody to set you free. Humble yourself and find somebody because you are going to get exposed anyway. But I've learned if you if you hold on to things and remain prideful, you are going to get exposed. God will expose you, especially if you want to serve him, yet you want to keep hiding your story. Humble yourself and watch God change your life.

HOW TO OVERCOME THE FEAR OF MAN

L et's talk about the fear of man. In Proverbs 29: 25, it says "Fearing people is a dangerous trap, but trusting the Lord means safety". We can obviously see based on this verse that if you fear man, you are going to be trapped. You are not going to move forward. You are not going to be able to do anything. What I have learned is fear will paralyze a person. Fear involves torment. If you fear anything, it will trap you. Whatever you fear, you become a slave to. Many times, when evangelizing, I get asked from people wanting to know how I can pray for people without worrying about what they think about me. The truth is the only way to overcome worry about what people think is to understand love. When you understand love and what it really means, you will not think about fear too often. God loves people and desires to encounter them; therefore, when you understand what this means you can overcome the fear. You are the outlet God wants to use. You will no longer worry about what a person thinks of you. You will not worry about if you are going to offend someone or do too much of this and too much of that. When you get into your mind and start overthinking, that is a sign that doubt, and unbelief is trying to set in which is all connected to fear. Fear paralyzes and when that starts to occur, it will take you down and prevent you from doing anything in life. There are people that literally lock themselves in houses because they are scared to go out and encounter other people. If I cared personally about what everybody thought about me, I would not be writing this book right now. I would not be doing half of the things God has me doing today including social media. I would not be doing anything because man's opinion will dictate everything I am doing. Listen, this is not to come across mean, but I cannot afford to care about what everyone thinks of me, and neither can you. If you are not doing anything to cause people to stumble and sin, then the opinions of man do not matter. I am doing the will of my heavenly father. When you are in the will of God, you can be confident that are fulfilling the great commission.

You enter into sin when you are not doing the things you are supposed to do. When you deal with self-doubt, self-hatred, rejection, and emotional stuff like, that it is when fear is produced. Fear of man is obviously produced by those attributes as well. Let's use our parents for example, when we grow up, we look to our parents for affirmation, encouragement, etc. Unfortunately, some of us never get away from that or our parents never release us, which causes our parents to be a hindering point to us. There are some people in their 30s and 40s still living by what their parents think of them. If I went by what my parents thought about me after I met Jesus, I would not be writing this book or traveling the world ministering the Gospel. Do not misunderstand, I still honor them in my holy disobedience towards God. Since I had left their home and no longer under that covering my path has been to follow wherever the Lord leads me, otherwise, I would not be doing what I am doing today. Many of you reading this book often get caught into familiar trends because we fear our parents the wrong way. I do not condone disobedience. I don't believe in dishonoring your parents. I believe we are supposed to honor them, but if they are telling you not to do the word of the Lord, you must obey God. You must do what God is telling you to do and you can do it respectfully by leaving their household if you are old enough. You can tell them that you love them, but you must do what you believe God is telling you to do.

When you examine the secular world, reflecting upon celebrities, actors, and musicians for example who achieved great accomplishments in life, they really advocate for the same thing. They will tell you that you cannot care about what people think. can't care what people think. If you really want to succeed and not be marginalizes, you cannot afford to care about what people think you. You got to move forward and go with the vision that God has giving you. The Bible says in Habakkuk 2:2 to write your vision down and make it plain. When you get a vision from God, the first thing that's going to try to stifle you is the fear of man. Everybody that was supposed to support you, suddenly, has come against you. When you get a vision, do not expect people to understand it. I used to tell people that I am going to be a Christian social media influencer. They laughed at me. I mean my family and others would laugh at me because they couldn't see it. I used to tell people that I am going to be a UFC champion. I was going to go all the way, and nothing was going to stop me. Now, Jesus stopped me because he wanted me to go down a different path, but people always doubted me. People would say Daniel you can't do this and that. Even Christian leaders would say Daniel you can't this and can't that. The things God has said to me either through dreams, visions, and directly placed in my heart, I went after no matter what people thought. I went through many battles, pain, tears, and experienced agony that most would never want to go through, all to get where I am today. Even with this mindset, I am not even close to where God is his wanting me to be in life. I am only tasting the beginning, the first fruits of it.

If you do not get consistency in your life, overstepping the boundaries of people, you will be able to harness what God has for you. People will always put boundaries in front of you. Be respectful and love to them yet tell them you respectfully disagree. Let them know that God has spoken to you, and they will see the fruits of it in due season. Joseph told his brothers his dream and they threw him in a pit to try to stop him. Let's just really think about this scenario. Have you ever told your friends or told your family members some of the things that God is going to do with you? Maybe you shared your dreams with a Christian leader. Has someone every laughed at your dream and told you that it won't happen or that you are crazy. I believe when people have a vision, if they are adhering to the principles of God, and go through their processes, that vision will manifest. Look God is not going to manifest your dream or vision overnight. There's a process, such as, character building that must happen first. Some people want it quick because they have an entitlement mentality. That's a whole different subject right there. Listen, if you embrace the processes that God wants to put you through, stay consistent, long suffering, possessing the fruits of the spirit, then you are going to get to where you need to go. I posted a comment recently that talks about the significant of being at the bottom of a mountain. When you are in the bottom of anything in life, you are going to have a whole support group with you as well. Everybody is ok with you when you are on equal playing ground with them. Can you agree with that? It is when you decide to break away from the bottom that people start to break away from you. Look at Joshua and Caleb for example. They were walking the same walk and saw the promised land. It was faith that prompted them to break away from others, despite their being giants ahead of them for them to possess the land. I'm sure people laughed at them too. They believed, according to God's promise, that they can have the land flowing with milk and honey. So, when you are at the bottom and then begin to start climbing to the top is when people start to scratch their heads. As you ascend the mountain of success and purpose that is when the stone throwers show up. Here comes the accusers of your past. Here comes the religious Pharisees. Here comes the family members that have always doubted you. Here comes everybody that never believed in you. Here comes the insecure people that refused to do what you are about to do. All the people that were at the bottom with you are now the ones throwing stones at you. But when you are in the bottom is when they could relate to you. They were your supporters. Now, this is where the fear of man steps in.

As you are ascending, the fear of man will start to speak to you. As you are walking up that mountain, the fear of man tries to make you think you are offending everybody. Oh look, you think you are better than everybody else. You need to go back down and humble yourself a little bit. You need to go back down there and be like them because you are you are making yourself look a certain way. Let me tell you something, if God is behind you, you are going to go up that mountain and they're going to stay down there running their mouth. I've learned that the ones who hate on me, who have always run their mouth, they are still at the bottom of the mountain running their mouth not going anywhere in life. If you are focused on what somebody else is doing, there's no way you can focus on what God wants you to do. If you are insecure, or jealous of another man or woman, you are going to focus on how you can destroy them. Your focus is going to be on how you can slow them down as they ascend the mountain. Now, if that person is focused on God's vision and purpose in their life, they will not care. Guess what? You won't be able to slow him down either. You can throw everything you want at them, and they will still succeed. Nobody can stop them.

The fear of man aims to step in and say things to get you to revert away from purpose. These are the defining moments of the Christian life. This is where you must mix in that love. The other very important thing that you must do is remove tolerance. You cannot mix love and tolerance all the time. Tolerance will pervert the love in your life. When you start to tolerate hate and the stones hitting you, that is when the stumbling and rolling back down the mountain starts to occur. You can love those people at a distance until they decide to repent and go up the mountain with you. Remember this, no one walking up the mountain should be stopping someone else from going up the mountain as well. A true leader wants everybody to go up the mountain. However, it is people that have doubt, self-hatred, and self-rejection, you will not be able to take them with you because they will slow you down. Understand that the fear of man steps in with the mission of stopping you from going up the mountain. Now, the fear of man has nothing to do with the people that were at the bottom of the mountain. The people at the bottom of the mountain are just talkers but the fear man comes in and wants to stop you. The fear of man is the voice of the devil that starts to speak. Consider Jesus, he was in the wilderness for 40 days and knew he had a mission to go to the cross. He knew he was going to be the most successful man that ever lived. He even told the disciples one time I'm going with or without you. I mean that is the militant mentality we all need. He asked if they were going or staying? Listen, a person that has vision from the Lord, nothing can stop them. That person cannot be stopped, not even by the people that supposedly support them. No Angel, demon, only God can do that.

There are some people whose goal is to tear me down. You might not witness it publicly, but in the background, these individuals exist. Do you want to know what my response is to these people? I tell them come on and throw the kitchen sink at me baby because you cannot stop what God said. If God said it, there's only one person who can stop it and that is God himself. Amen. Jesus knew the only person that could ever stop Him was the father in heaven and He knew the father never goes back on His promises. God doesn't repent of what He said. He said Jesus you are going to come and save mankind. You are going to be that ultimate sacrifice that everybody's been needing. You are going to go to that cross and die a gruesome death. It is going to be crazy, but the reward of being the king of the Kingdom that I want to establish on this earth is put into your hands. All mankind is going to worship me through you. Wow, isn't that wonderful? He is the expressed image of the father in heaven. Bless Jesus, seriously, because He has giving up everything for us. If Jesus would have said in the garden of Gethsemane, when he was crying tears of blood, that He does not want to through the cup of suffering, we would not be where we are today. Jesus instead stayed firm no matter the weight, the pressure, and the stones that came again Him.

Now, does this all have to do with the fear of man? The answer is yes. The Bible says in Proverbs 29:25 that "The fear of man lays a snare, but whoever trusts in the Lord is safe". What is a snare? It is a trap. Another translation refers to it as a 'dangerous' trap because it will hold you back. You know some people live to be 80 or 90 years old, stuck in the same snare. They live that long and then experience one divine moment near the end of their life and realize that they have been trapped in a snare for too long. No one reading this book should want to be trapped. Nobody should want to be snared to fear. Nobody should want to be stared to depression, self-hatred, and self-rejection. You don't want your foot to be stuck in this. Some of the things you are going through today all you need do is make a move. All you have to do is move your feet. Well, Daniel that looks dangerous. That looks crazy. Should I really do that? Yes, do it. Does it involve risk? If it involves risk which requires faith, that is what's going to get you from glory to glory and faith to faith.

Does it take refinement? Is it going to change your character? Is it going to make you better, than do it? You must make a move and can't wait on the next prophetic word to come to you. Look, I just prophesied to you. Many of us receive a prophetic word, and then we wait for an angel to appear and push us forward, not knowing that it doesn't take faith. Anytime Jesus saw a person come after him, he would say 'O, ye of great faith'. Faith moves the heart of God. Faith is the overcomer of fear. Faith will take you out of the fear of man. If you are out evangelizing and hear the Lord say pray for that person's knee, you know what usually happens? You will begin to hear things like 'oh, you better not" or 'just pray for them later'. You will even think to yourself if they come around again, you'll pray for them at that time. All these thoughts will come to you in efforts to try to stop you from touching a life. These are opportunities to operate in obedience because that person could be holding the key to your next thing with Jesus. So, go and you can pray for that person who has that infirmity or disease because they can unlock your next opportunity with God. I've seen that happen so many times in my life. Do you guys know what got me where I am right now in life? Simple evangelism. Sometimes I would go out when no one knew. I would go out to the campuses, into the streets, fellowship with teenagers, and feed the homeless. I became the evangelist of a church. I did all these things which I believe has led me to where I am today. If you are faithful in little, you will be faithful in much.

I am not an overnight sensation. See people look at the success and fail to see the journey. Anyone that I have seen become an overnight sensation typically does not have the character to maintain it. Look at the one hit wonders in life. They didn't have the wisdom and the discernment to be able to handle the success that was given to them. That's why getting things fast is not always a good thing. Think about people that hit the lottery, they waste their money quick because they don't understand things like taxes. I mean they don't understand what it means to go into another tax bracket. In fact, many of you reading this book do not know much about the various tax brackets. If you want to be a successful, you will need learn this type of stuff. This is very important information for people who people who want to be successful in the Kingdom. These are people are people who do not want to be poor minded for the rest of their life. The fear of man will keep you in a deprived state. I believe the world is in the state that it is in today because Christians are asleep, refusing to take on the mountain top journey. I believe a lot of Christians have become comfortable just sitting in the church and not wanting to be anything in life. Man, I was never comfortable just sitting in the pews doing nothing. I always knew something had to be done to change matters around me, let alone the world. Of course, I could learn, teach, and be taught, but if the church won't move into the things of God, I'm ready to move outside. People would follow me into the streets. Pastors tend to get jealous when they see a man or woman of God doing radical things because they aren't yet should be. Even worse, sometimes they will persecute you for doing the work of the Lord. Overall, you want to be in a place where the river is constantly flowing. It doesn't say a pond of God, but a river. We're in the river of God that is always moving and flowing.

Ultimately, people that have the fear of man on their life are not in a flow. You can always tell when people are affected by the fear of man. Nothing successful is happening to them. The voice of man is going to enable the fear of man in your life because you are going to be led by their affections and opinions. Unfortunately, you do not know what comes with that. Man will try to give you their worldly carnal wisdom birthed from a jealous place. It can sound like God and not be God. It could be birthed from jealousy and envy. Think about the story of old which is why you need to read your bible. that's why you need to read your Bible. Think of the story about the new and old prophets. Do you know that because the new prophet listened to the old prophet causing the new prophet to get ate by a lion? Sometimes when God is doing a new thing you can't listen to those who came before you. It is important to have discernment because you must be able to know what type of person to listen to. Of course, honor those who came before you. Of course, if the man of God is a true father, or the woman of God is a true mother, listen to them. What I am emphasizing is that you must make sure that you understand the word of God and have discernment. You also do not want to have rebellion in your heart either. You must ensure that you are reading the word, spending time in prayer, and you have discernment so that you know who is speaking to you. Read the story of David and Saul. If Saul had his way, David would have been shut down. Saul was jealous and envious of David. Again, it is important that know who you are standing before because if you are dictated by man's opinions, you will be dictated by their emotions which can come from a bad place. If they are not led by the Holy Spirit, they will try to slow you down.

I celebrate the men and women of God who are there working because I know it is their portion and their assignment. My heart for forerunners is that everyone succeeds. I believe everybody eats. If you never heard that term before, it just means that everyone should benefit. That was the heart of the apostles in the book of Acts. Everybody should eat which means, there should be no poverty and lack. This is how we are supposed to be in the Kingdom; however, that is not reality. Some people do not get over certain struggles. The fear of man is a dangerous trap. My prayer for everyone reading this book is that today you get free from that spirit.

Now, I am going to tell you how to not get entangled in in the fear of man. In Mark 12:30-31, it says "And you shall love the Lord you God with all your heart and with all your soul and with all your mind and with all your strength. The second is this, you shall love your neighbor as yourself. There is no other commandment greater than these". Loving God with everything in your being is the key to overcoming the fear of man. When you love God, you love his ways, his commandments, what he stands for, and character. You must also love your neighbor as yourself. Let me tell you something very important. If you don't love yourself, you are going to love the opinions of the man who is speaking to you which means you can be seduced, turned left and right. People can trick you and flipped upside down all the way till Sunday. You need to make sure you love yourself and the way you love yourself is by loving what God created.

I travel all over the United States and encounter people who do not forgive themselves. These are people who do not love themselves because they're living in the past. They are trapped by the fear of man because they offended somebody on the way up and their foot. Look, we all make mistakes. We all go through things, but if you keep living in the past, you are going to be trapped. Again, the fear of man is going to trap you. You are going to held down because you cannot love yourself. You are going to be looking at yourself consistently and wanting to self-improve all the time. There's nothing wrong with wanting to be better, but you can't fix yourself in your own strength. It is impossible. When I notice something about myself, I'll sit down, pray and I'll ask for the grace of God. You must sit down and ask for God's grace. I was going through a season where I was trying to get my weight down to 220 from 260. I told the Lord that I cannot do this by myself because I have no self-control with food. I need your grace. I asked the Lord for Grace, and you know what happened to me without me dwelling it on it for too long, I have received self-control. I had grace on my life which helped me lose weight. Grace empowers change. If you have God's grace on a situation, it will empower you to be able to overcome that thing you are suffering with in life. Ask yourself have you asked for God's grace regarding a certain sins or struggle in your life? Have you asked for God's grace to overcome it? Jesus overcame the world. He overcame sin. Why are you continuing to look for the next modality or sermon? God has simply given the answer to you through his son Jesus Christ.

In 1 John 4:18 -19 says this "There is no fear in love, but perfect love casts out fear. For fear involves torment, but he who fears has not been perfected in love. We love because e first loved us". Right here in this passage it says if love is present, you can't have fear because there is no fear in love. Perfect love casts out fear. Do you understand love? Have you asked God for an encounter with His love? Have you asked Him for a baptism of his love? Aren't you tired of being dictated by what people think or will say about you?

You need love to rid yourself of fear. Please understand this when you go out to evangelize, start a business, or anything God is calling you to do in life. Know the voice of God and the voice of the enemy. If you know how the voice of your father speaks, then guess what? You are going to do as your father says. Jesus only did as his father instructed Him. He said 'I 'm about my father's business'. He knew how his father spoke as well when the adversary was speaking. How do you know how the father speaks? Spend time with Him. Jesus said, 'My sheep know my voice and they will not listen to the voice of another'. And here's the beautiful thing, if you do have a moment of listening to the voice of another, you can always repent. Jesus Christ can put you back on that narrow path that leads the life. Remember, we're not in this to gain popularity and prestige. We're here to gain souls. God wants there to be godly business owners, politicians, and preachers to name a few. He wants godly everything. Just know that God wants to see you walk in your divine assignment free from the fear of man.

How to Overcome the Fear of Man

HOW TO AVOID SIN

Oftentimes when I am out and about praying for folks, I see what I call repeat offenders. They are repeat offenders because they keep doing the same thing. It is like a prison term. What I notice is that people often will go back to their vomit. You know they will go back like a dog returns to the vomit. People will often go back to their old ways. I believe the reason this happens is because they really have not grasped what it means to repent from their sin. I do not think they understand how the sin originated nor the weight of it. Why shouldn't we sin? Why should we walk away from it? Oftentimes people don't get it. I receive hundreds of messages from people who are suffering from various things. I get it, demons and strongholds are there but they had to get in through an access point. I want to provide you with wisdom and knowledge to cut off the access point so that you aren't suffering with sin.

If you want to overcome sin, you must know it's origin. Why is sin bad? Why does sin cause so many problems? Why does the bible say to flee from it and not partake of it? Let's examine its origin. Some would say that the original sin started in the garden with Adam and Eve but, it did not. The sin mankind committed started in the garden, but it was Satan who committed the first sin. Lucifer was the first sinner. In the book of Isaiah 14:12-14, it says "How you are fallen from heaven, O Lucifer, son of the morning! How are you a cut down to the ground, you who weakened the nations! For you have said in your heart, 'I will ascend into heaven, I will exalt my throne above the stars of God; I will also sit on the mount of congregation on the farthest sides of the north; I will ascend above the heights of the clouds, I will be like the Most-High'". There you go...pride which was the creation of sin right there. Oh, Lucifer said to himself that He will like his creator. He aimed to ascend above the heights of the clouds and have a throne above God. This is when lunacy entered in. Crazy psychotic sin entered his heart. Lucifer is a created being. He is an angel who had remarkable musical capabilities. He was probably a good-looking angel that had it going on, decked out in jewels. Somehow his capabilities went to his head. Maybe he was an angel that others marveled at. Have you ever said to someone don't let a compliment go to your head? Well, Lucifer let it go to his head and that he set his heart to go against God which got him cast out of heaven. What did Jesus say? I saw Satan fall like lightning. Lucifer fell from the top and went straight to the bottom.

Pride comes before destruction and a haughty spirit before a fall. Some people say pride comes before a fall, but destruction precedes pride. I have dealt with pride in my own life. I believe we all have suffered with symptoms of pride. They get revealed as we seek the Lord and as we move forward in the anointing. When pride is revealed, it causes us to go from glory to glory and faith to faith. If we humble ourselves and lose dignity before the Lord, he will be faithful to deliver us. and he'll be faithful to let us go from faith to faith and glory to glory. Sin I have found always roots itself in pride and another name for pride is self-worship, or the worship of self. If there's a lot of self involved, pride is someone near. If there is a lot of "I this and me that", there is self-worship or pride involved. Pay attention to those words in a lot of young preachers. I am still young although I have been in ministry for over 10 years. I started preaching at 23 and traveling the nations at 25. Many young preachers who are anointed suffer with pride and must be broken. It sounds bad, but it is true. You know you can be 40 years old, meet the Holy Spirit for the first time, and go straight into Pride City because the power of God started to move through you. The Holy Spirit will use anybody but remember character, the resistance of pride, is up to us and our obedience to the Lord. I am not saying that if you are a new believer that you are going to suffer with pride. Don't misunderstand. What I am trying to explain is that based on my experience, people usually have to be broken when they first come to the Lord. The process of breaking results in your vessel being able to leak good oil. The only way to get oil out of an olive is to crush it. Consider a wine press which involves stepping on grapes to extract the juice. A crushing is always required when you go from glory to glory and faith to faith. Embrace the crushing when you first come to the Lord, baptized in the Holy Spirit. The crushing process can take years. The killing of pride in a man's life can take quite a while.

A prophet that I once knew who has since gone on to be with the Lord told me that the making of a prophet takes many years. He said to become a well-seasoned prophet usually occurs when you are between 40-60 years old. Of course, that is if you started out in ministry early in life. Overall, it takes some time to for God to really season a person. We are all prideful in the beginning because we were born into a sinful state. We have a selfish nature that has to be crushed for the glory of God. God is faithful to help us in our time of need. He is just a good father because He shows us our ways and lead us to accept Him. I just love him. You know when it hurts, it is good. I've learned that when something in you is hurting because God is taking something out of your life, get out of His way and let it happen. I know it hurts in the moment but accept it.

Lucifer was the first sinner; however, when sin first entered through man it occurred with Adam and Eve. Everybody knows the story of Genesis. God gave Adam and Eve one thing not to do and it was that very thing that they ended up doing. As a result, sin came in. The Lord God took man and put him in the garden of Eden to tend and keep it. He commanded the man to eat from every tree of the garden freely but not the tree of the knowledge of good and evil. He further states that the day that you eat of it you shall surely die. We know that the wages of sin is death. God gave a very clear and direct commandment to Adam and Eve which is to touch that tree. God was so gracious to allow them to eat from everything else. I mean can you imagine the paradise they resided in? God knew that if they ate of it, it would corrupt them. He knew that it would give them knowledge that they do not need. He knew that it would take their focus off Him. Of course, if we read further in the book of Genesis, we see where Adam and Eve ate from the forbidden tree.

Now in Genesis 3:1 it says, "Now the serpent was more cunning than any beast of the field which the Lord God had made. And he said to the woman, 'Has God indeed said, you shall not eat of every tree of the garden'." You see right there that is a seducing spirit trying to entice her into doing something that she shouldn't. Verse 2-4 says "And the woman said to the serpent, 'We may eat the fruit of the trees of the garden, but of the fruit of the tree, which is in the midst of the garden, God has said. You shall not eat it, nor shall you touch it, lest you die. Then the serpent said to the woman, you will not surely die'." This reminds me of when Jesus spent 40 days in the desert because Satan tried to twist God's words there as well. He has been using the same tactics over and over. Verse 5 says "For God knows that in that day you eat of it your eyes will be opened, and you will be like God". Now, there is the temptation. Eat the fruit and you are going to become just like God. You can become God pretty much which is what the serpent was saying. Verse 6 says "So when the woman saw that the tree was good for food, that it was pleasant to the eyes, and a tree desirable to make one wise, she took of its fruit and ate". Another important note here is that when Satan offers you something, it will look good. It will look desirable. It will bring a lust out of you for it. It drives you towards that thing; however, because it looks good, that does not mean it's from God. Paul said all things are permissible, but not all things are good. We must be discerning because the serpent is crafty.

In your personal time, dissect the book of Genesis 3:1 to 7. Please know that there is a serpent who is always whispering. If he knows he cannot get in your ear, he is going to try to send it through somebody else. Look, I've been bamboozled plenty of times in Christianity. I am still learning how that little crafty snake works. I've seen him in ministry come against marriages. In my past, I've seen him give me some uppercuts, take my shoes, and steal everything from me. So, I've been seduced before by this serpent and that is why I have a hatred for sin now. Some people wonder how I am able to walk in authority like I do. It is because I have been bit and I am not going to get bit again by this serpent. He's always trying to get us to bite; therefore, we must always be wise. The bibles says that we should be wise as serpents and harmless as doves. Why does it say wise as a serpent? Because you have to think like your enemy. You have to know your enemy. Some people say don't focus on the devil. Focus on Jesus because you become the enemy. Let me reveal something to you, one of the things Satan wants you to do is to think that he has no power and doesn't exist. Look at this earth. He is the prince of the power of the air. He has a level of authority that has been given to him on this earth. Now, he can't touch us. He can affect us when we are found in Christ, praying, and have a relationship with God. The moment that you forget he exists; is the moment he can strike pretty hard. My eyes are open, and I know I'm in warfare. I know the spirit realm is real and I do not by God's grace want to be seduced by that sneaky serpent any longer. I went through a moment in my life where I lost everything to the seductions of that serpent. Please be wise and know your enemy. Satan walks around like a roaring lion, looking to devour who he can. Note that he walks around "like" a roaring lion, not that he is one. So, there must be a legality to who he can touch and who he can affect.

Eve ATE of the fruit and then gave to Adam to eat it as well. Adam should have stood up and said "No!", but he didn't. He became a passive man, partaking of the fruit when he knew it was wrong. After they ate, both of their eyes became opened, and they knew they were naked. They instantly became aware of their flesh and carnality. The sin nature has now entered, and the flesh is alive. Now, because of all of this, Jesus had to come and completely restore what the enemy stole from man. Jesus is the second Adam. We need to be transformed by the renewing of our mind to discern the perfect and acceptable will of God for our lives.

We just need to accept the cross.

Let's discuss the weight of sin. In Romans 6:23, it says "For the wages of sin is death, but the gift of God is eternal life in Christ Jesus our Lord". Sin will always lead you to death. Anything that is not done in faith is sin. If you choose sin, expect consequences for that sin. if you go. For example, if you are in a marriage and become disloyal, there is a consequence that will result in brining someone pain. It is going to cause damage to your family and oftentimes the most vulnerable which is children. If you decide to steal from a bank, it is highly likely unless by God's grace, you are probably going to jail. God has been known to open jail cells so anything can happen because he is a redeemer and a restorer. Ultimately, if you are alive, you will always have a way to turn things around, but there is a consequence to sin. I was telling someone recently I don't care if you are a Buddhist, Muslim, Atheist, or Christian, there are spiritual laws in place that no one can change. Whatever you sow, that will be what you reap. The beautiful thing is that we have Jesus Christ who is the way, the truth, and the life. He is the only way out of our cages. He is the only way out of our prisons. The wages of sin is death. Now, there are spiritual laws God put in place that cannot be altered and the only way to overcome is to accept Jesus Christ who has fulfilled the law. When you look at the one who has fulfilled the law, you no longer need to focus on all the ordinances and things associated because Jesus has fulfilled it. Some of you are probably scratching your head trying to understand what this all means. You must know about the old and new covenant in the Bible. You must understand law and grace. Grace empowers us to overcome sin and to change. Do I believe we can be completely sin free? I believe Jesus is completely sin free and when we set our gaze upon Him, we no longer have to worry about being a sinner. If you do sin, Jesus is the propitiation of our sins.

When we refuse to repent, sometimes the Lord will allow us, in our pride and destructive carnal thinking, to feel the weight of a sin. He will do that to prevent us from wanting to touch it again. We are like hardheaded kids with stiff a neck. We touched the hot stove once, we touch it again, and eventually your hand starts to burn off before you realize that you shouldn't touch it again. There is a weight to sin that we must hate and release from our lives. We must understand what Jesus has done for us at the cross of Calvary. When he said, "It is finished", it changed everything. Do we realize what we have obtained through his sacrifice? If we did, we wouldn't want sin anymore.

How do we avoid sin? There are 4 simple ways to avoid sin. Number 1, you must except Jesus Christ's life given sacrifice on the cross to become saved and born again. According to John 3:16, it says, "For God so loved the world that he gave his one and only son that the world would not perish but everybody would come to have eternal life through him". Isn't that wonderful? You must be born again. Getting water baptized is a representation of being born again. How did you come out of your mom when she gave birth? You came out through a sack of water. Being born again is a representation of coming out of the water again.

Number 2, become filled with the Holy Spirit. Very important to become filled with the Holy Ghost because it empowers you to beat the wiles of the devil. You can walk in power of God. The baptism of the Holy Spirit also increases the conviction of sin in your life. He will speak to you and give you supernatural wisdom and discernment of how the enemy operates. He'll show you what the devil is cooking up and how to not only maneuver around his schemes but destroy it. The Holy Spirit will give you a way out constantly because you have the power that rose Jesus from the grave on the inside of you. It is a necessity in your Christian walk to be filled with the Holy Spirit. I think that's why Christians live like hell going to heaven because they don't get filled with the Holy Ghost. Be filled with the Holy Ghost so that you can live at full capacity. When you are filled with the Holy Spirit, the enemy can attack you and you will not get offended. You can stand firm and become like Christ in those situations. Only through the Holy Spirit can you do that. Only through the Holy Spirit can you walk in the path of God because it increases the conviction of sin in your life. I've noticed when I got filled with the Holy Spirit, and truly surrendered, I got delivered from a lot of stuff. The baptism of the Holy Spirit caused me to have a stronger, deeper remorse, and conviction towards sin. The Bible says in 2 Corinthians 7:10 that "Godly sorry brings repentance that leads to salvation and leaves no regret, but worldly sorrow brings death". Godly sorrow will come when you have the Holy Ghost. It allows you recognize when you have grieved Him. You will feel the weight of hurting God's heart.

Number 3, build your relationship with God by reading His word and fellowshipping with Jesus through His spirit. In other words, develop your prayer life. I'm in constant unceasing prayer. I'm aware of my King at all times. Develop your prayer life which is the key and reading His word. When you want to know or become like someone, you have a desire to hang around that individual. People desire to be used in ministry; either a prophet, preacher, or evangelist to name a few. You will not be able to do any of that if you do not know His word or how to serve the Lord appropriately. It is powerful and a good start by just telling someone that Jesus loves them, but you need feed on the word of God if you are going to be able to provide them more substance. The Lord wants us to go deeper into understanding and consuming His word. Do you want to cast out demons with authority? Listen demons recognize people who know the King. They know if you are spending time with the One they hate because then they start to hate you. Demons will freak out when they get close to you.

Remember the sons of Sceva. Demons chased them out wounded and naked because they didn't know them; in other words, they didn't have a relationship with Jesus. They knew about Paul but did not know them. Build your relationship with God by reading His word and fellowshipping with Jesus through His spirit. Once you begin doing this, I assure you things are going to be awesome. You will fall in love with Him. You'll have waves of His glory and anointing come upon you. It is the most amazing thing to experience. It is totally the precious and wonderful presence of Jesus Christ.

Number 4, become obedient through the above steps. Fall madly in love with your creator. Fall in love with him. If you do the things outlined in this chapter, you will end up loving God's ways, and you will understand that they are sustainment to everything in this life. You will also fall in love with mankind. You will be able to love your neighbor. You can do this because you understand that God loves Him. Remember in doing this you are fulfilling two commandments which is loving God with all your heart, mind, and soul, and love your neighbor as yourself. You don't really have a choice; you have to love you.

These are keys on how to avoid sin. This is how you win the battle. The results will be you are Kingdom minded and living life as a true citizen of heaven. We pray often for healing, miracles, signs, and wonders, but if we do not get the revelation that sin is destructive, and to turn away from it, we are not embracing the full gospel. Embrace and preach the full gospel. Pay close attention to any preacher that operates in great signs and anointings but do not preach against sin. You want to make sure whoever you are following, they're pointing you back to Jesus Christ, the true healer and deliverer. All glory belongs to Jesus Christ.

HOW TO LIVE IN THE SPIRIT

I think it is very important in this day to learn how to truly walk in the spirit. If you do not know how to walk int the spirit you will be deceived and given over to any wind of crazy doctrine. If you do not have a relationship with the Holy Spirit, you are going to have hard time discerning what is God and what isn't. There are many voices arising in this hour, and it is important that the body of Christ is not deceived. If the doctrine isn't sound, if it doesn't line up with the word of God, if there is compromise in it, run far away because it is not from God. God's word is absolute truth. God's word is unchanging, and His grace is the same as His mercies. Jesus said, "I am the same yesterday, today, and forever". He is the only thing that is absolute.

People change daily. Our emotions can make us switch at the drop of a hat. The beautiful thing is that Jesus's emotions are always the same towards us. His will is good and perfect for us. He has something amazing prepared for us. In Jeremiah 20 it mentions God having a plan and purpose for our lives. A future and a hope are what He has bestowed upon us. He has something great in store. So, the question becomes how do we live in the spirit? The first thing we must do to live in the spirit is to be born right of the spirit or what we say be born again. I discuss this extensively in the previous chapter. We cannot walk in the spirit if we are not born again. We can't even fathom what walking in the spirit means. If you tell a person that's walking in the flesh to begin walking in the spirit, they're going to look at you like you are crazy. Why is that? Because they haven't been born again. They will not understand. You can't tell a carnal man to walk in the spirit. It is impossible.

You cannot judge them because they're walking in ignorance. They have no revelation of the state they are in until the Holy Spirit comes upon them, and they're born of water and spirit. Take a minute and reflect on the moment you accepted Jesus. The moment you became born again and everything changed. Your consciousness changed, your awareness of things around you, your convictions, and more all changed. change a lot of things. It is just a whole different world compared to where we came from. Things changing is also a good sign that you are born again. If you know what it means to walk by the spirit and you understand it, there's a good chance you are born again. On the flip side, you will not understand what I'm if you do not have the Holy Spirit. Spirit bears witness to spirit.

In John, 3:56 it says, "Jesus replied, I assure you no one can enter the Kingdom of God without being born of water and the spirit. Humans can reproduce only human life, but the Holy Spirit gives birth to spiritual life". Right here it tells us that flesh gives birth to flesh and spirit gives birth to spirit. Number 2, when we choose to live by the spirit, we do not feed the desires of our flesh. Being led by our fleshly desires results in death and destruction; however, being led by the spirit leads us to life and truth. When you are living by the spirit, when your flesh rises, you feel conviction if you are one who walks in the spirit. In Romans 8:14 it says, "For whoever is led by the spirit of God, they are the sons of God". When you are led by the spirit you don't want to fulfill the desires of the flesh. If you are one who allows your flesh to lead, it will eventually eat you alive. Therefore, we see Christians who are filled with the Holy Spirit yet have demons. Convictions are like sirens that go off so that you can know that you are in danger to turnaround and go down the right path. Christians who hear those sirens end up running somewhere for freedom because they do not want to live in sin and be demonized. When you are walking by the spirit you cannot feed the desires of your flesh. The conviction is too strong, even backslidden Christians become tormented because they know that they cannot fulfill that fleshly desire. The Holy Spirit is in a constant place of convicting backsliders of sin in hopes of restoring the prodigal back to Himself. Once you have been born again, you cannot go back and live the old life. If you do, you can be given over to a reprobate mind. A reprobate mind is an unprincipled, morally deprived individual who because of their sin God has rejected due to wickedness. If you go back to sin, you are literally saying I knew the spirit and I want nothing to do with it which is a dangerous place to be. You don't want to get in that place as a Christian. But most times Christians have tasted the goodness of the Holy Spirit, they know better than to go out there and enjoy feeding the desires of the flesh. If you are falling into sin as a Christian and feel convicted that is a good thing. If there's no conviction, that is a bad place to be therefore, you need to pray for conviction to come into your life. When you are battling with a sin that you hate and don't want to engage in, but cannot seem to break, that is a struggle. A struggle is different from willful sinning. Jesus knows how to make a way where there is no way. He knows how to make the crooked paths straight, even if you fall seven times, you'll get back up. He will always give us a way out. Think about the children of Israel who were in the desert for 40 years. God finally gave them a way out. You might be around a mountain or desert a long time, I assure you there is always a way out. Again, when we choose to live by the spirit, we do not have want to feed the desires of the flesh. Our flesh leads us into death and destruction but being led by the spirit leads us to life and truth.

In Galatians 5:16 it says, "I say then, walk in the Spirit, and you shall not fulfill the lust of the flesh". The sinful nature wants to do evil, which is opposite of what the spirit wants for us. These two forces are constantly fighting each other. When you are a directed by the spirit, you are not under obligation by the law of Moses. When you follow desires of the sinful nature, the results are very clear. Here are some keys to know if you are being led by your flesh. You are engaged in sexual immorality, impurity, sorcery, hostility, quarreling jealousy, outbursts of the anger, selfish ambition, dissension, division, envy, drunkenness, wild parties, and other sins like these. Let me tell you again, as I have before that. Anyone living a sinful life will not inherit the Kingdom of

God. You can't. The Holy Spirit produces fruits in our lives that indicates that we are walking in the spirit. Those fruits are love, joy peace, patience, kindness, goodness, faithfulness, gentleness, and self-control. There is no law which is a beautiful thing. This is how you don't get bound by the law and the condemnation of the law. There is no law against the fruits of the Spirit. Those who belong to Christ have nailed the passions and desires of their sinful nature to his cross and crucified them there.

There are two things that I talk to people about and that is living by the law and living by the spirit. Many may not realize this but when Jesus came, the Pharisees were putting heavy yokes and legalistic standards on people. They were forcing the people to uphold the legalistic standards of the law which resulted in them living in a condemned state. Unfortunately, they were never able to come to truly know their God, because the Pharisees became a stumbling block between them and God. The Pharisees presented themselves as being righteous in the eyes of man. They positioned themselves before the people as being the only ones capable of reaching God. Jesus came to abolish those legalistic restrictions. He called them out for being dirty on the inside; lustful, self-righteous, and not really knowing God. Jesus exemplified before the people the true character of God.

My prayer for everyone reading this book is that we come to truly know our heavenly father. My prayer is that we remain in a place of needing our father and savior in our life. If you feel like the weight of life is too great for you to handle, then give it to God. Jesus literally said, "Cast your burdens upon me". Cast your cares upon the Him and don't carry the heavy yokes and burden of life. This is not what God intended for mankind. If you are waking up every day expecting to sin and mess up, if you are offended, and scared, then you are under the law. You are under a legalistic standard that you cannot uphold. The beautiful thing is you can turn from it and walk and live by the law of the spirit. The Holy Spirit is the comforter. He teaches you things as you go. For those of you who have children, when they make a mistake how do you handle it? You want to walk them how not to make the mistake again. You teach them how to do things appropriately. Why? Because you love them, and you want them to succeed in life. Our heavenly father loves us more than you can imagine. The important aspect of learning a lesson is being able to hear it. You must know the voice of God. To recognize His voice, you must know Him through His word. Faith is also required to know God, and if you know Him by faith, you will know that He will never leave nor forsake you. He will be with you always even until the end of the world.

When I went through my victim stage in life, I got to a point where I couldn't stand it any longer. I used to blame others for my hardships. Eventually, I had to go back and right my wrongs because I knew that I could not be led by the spirit until I released people from my heart. There are tests and trials that will come into your life. They will come to test if you really released unforgiveness, offense, and resentment in your heart. Make sure you completely release everything that is not like God from your heart. Don't hold on to the burdens which are yokes because God wants all of us to live in the spirit consistently. He wants us to be Holy Ghost walkers ensuring every step is led by the Holy Spirit. God is not expecting perfection, but he is expecting us to learn the lesson that leads to perfection.